THE AMERICAN ENTERPRISE PARTY

I0096617

Volume III

Restore the American Work Ethic with Humanism

JERRY RHOADS
Founder and CEO

THE AMERICAN ENTERPRISE PARTY

Volume III

Restore the
American
Work Ethic
with Humanism

JERRY RHOADS
Founder and CEO

Printed in the United States of America
ISBN:
        Softcover   979-8-9910186-2-3
        eBook

Published by: Rhoads Publishing
Publication Date: 06/25/2024

THE AMERICAN ENTERPRISE PARTY

Volume III

Restore the
American
Work Ethic
with Humanism

JERRY RHOADS
Founder and CEO

Printed in the United States of America
ISBN:
        Softcover   979-8-9910186-2-3
        eBook

Published by: Rhoads Publishing
Publication Date: 06/25/2024

PREFACE

AMERICANISM MISSION STATEMENT

In America we now have two tribes fighting each other and losing the American Dream. The Left and the Right forgo the middle American voter, for one-party control. A THIRD-PARTY SWING VOTE that breaks ties, does cost-benefit analysis for accountability, and keeps the money-tics and partisan politics honest in operating the Great America Enterprise profitably. Using generally accepted accounting principles GAAP for reporting the financial condition of the Republic. By being the referee for consensus cost via benefit decisions making to avoid one-party control and bankruptcy. In God we trust, when Monetary Capitalists share and Human Socialists care, and where the free market enterprise is truly laissez-faire.

THAT'S WHAT MAKES AMERICA ENTERPRISE GREAT,

WITH THE CHALLENGE OF GLOBAL TRADE.

WE NEED PEACEFUL COEXISTENCE DETENTE TO,

KEEP AMERICAN ENTERPRISE RETURN ON OUR COLLATERAL GREAT.

PEACE THROUGH STRENGTH IS A STRONG ECONOMIC BASE (COST OF SALES AND OVERHEAD), ROI, CASH FLOW, AND NON-PROLIFERATION OF NUCLEAR WEAPONS OF MASS DESTRUCTION.

"We the people expect all American citizens to ask not, what you can do for your party. Ask what you can do for your own American Dream."

WHAT THE STATUTE OF LIBERTY REPRESENTS

(Not Blinded by the Light of the Benjamin Might)

Americanism the process of American monetary capitalism merged with American Socialism produces laissez-faire market enterprise, profits, capital, ROI, and cash flow. Financed by our system of laissez-faire competitive, color-blind economics. Human capital, the skills, knowledge, and experience invested in laissez-faire enterprise drives collective wealth.

$E=mc2$ ... Enterprise = monetary capital times human capital squared = profit, cash flow, ROI in GDP, and GNP. Economics = cost of sales and budgetary spending and deficits = +/- spendable surplus for research and development that drives national growth and prosperity.

What do the scales of Lady Justice represent?

The balance (scales) represents weighing facts, and evidence to decide a verdict. It also shows her duty to restore balance to society. Although many people think of Lady Justice as wearing a blindfold, she can also be shown without one. Both versions highlight her impartiality. The rule of law prevents the law of rulers and regulators.

BLINDED BY THE BENJIMAN'S MIGHT. Ask not what you can do for your party. Ask what you can do for your country.   THE AMERICAN ENTERPRISE PARTY TRILOGY

AMERICANISM AND HUMANISM ARE THE AMERICAN DREAM

VOLUME ONE: THE MISSION OF AMERICANISM

VOLUME TWO: THE QUASI-REORGANIZATION OF DEBT AND DEFICITS

VOLUME THREE: RESTORE AMERICAN WORK ETHIC WITH HUMANISM

The America Dream's American Enterprise Rhoads theorem E=mc2

Laissez-faire enterprise equals American Monetary capital times Human capital squared.
AMERICANISM = American Capitalism gestated by American Socialism multiplies prosperity to be shared by the shareholders, human capital, and stakeholders.
The Ten Tenets of Laissez-fair enterprise.
This formula works daily in all American businesses, small, medium, and large international enterprises.

Tenets of American Laissez-Faire Enterprise:

It's a world of competitive global forces attacking our values and internally woke reasons for changing our way of life. It's a war of doubt and fear won with faith and leadership standing up for the 10 tenets of American Laissez-faire. Then the American Dream tenets of the Many are one result of each American striving for a quality of life.

1) Reward received is determined by the amount of risk taken. Protected by US bankruptcy laws and the rule of law.

2) The law of supply and demand for measuring markets.

3) Sharing is based on the skill to bill and the risk taken to produce goods and services creating GDP and GNP.

4) Earning is based on risk taken by learning a skill to bill for goods and services. Profits.

5) Competition creates optimal quality, innovation, and cash flow from GDP/GNP creating retained earnings for capital growth and reinvestment.

6) Quality creates cost savings and profits. Profits create growth. And capital for R&D and market expansion.

7) GAAP reports actual financial and operational results. Stock and bond markets report derivatives.

8) USA Debt clock and financial analytics are based on GAAP, a guideline for collective prosperity based on the cost of sales, profits, and cash flow.

9) USA balance sheet, sustainability is a current ratio of two times current assets and current debt, including accruals for future obligations, less than 85% of GDP and GNP.

10) Accountability for the above 9 tenets is the bottom line for measuring leadership. It's cashflow rewarding shareholders, funding workers for profit sharing, stakeholders for benevolent, and capital growth. Where shareholders share and stakeholders receive donations, not profits.

American Enterprise is not Woke capitalism or socialism. It's a free-market enterprise Capitalism (money) managed by Socialism (workers) for the prosperity of its investors practicing the above 10 tenets. Nor is there a need for a FREE-MARKET enterprise to practice or use the ESG index (environmental – social – governance) for evaluating Governance. That is done by www.usdebtclock.org, www.nationaldebtclock.org GDF.

GNP, GAAP, and the WORLD global marketplace.

Supported by keeping the dollar as the reference currency as asset based in global trade exchange rates based on the power of the USA collateral reported by the www.usdebtclock.org
:

Precious metal reserves	$ 1,221,800,000,000
Mineral reserves	$ 5,701,800,000,000
Real Estate	$75,344,400,000,000
Land	$24,502,000,000,000
Stock Market	$50,908,000,000,000
Recaptured assets	$ 7,537,000,000,000
New energy	$ 3,970,000,000,000
Total USA collateral	$169,187,000,000,000
Per citizen	$503,700

Increasing at a trillion per month based on E=mc2.

This dwarfs the old gold standard for debt and deficit backing. The problem is liquidity, and the American Enterprise Party proposes additional capital, not using taxation but Trade War Bonds to support the Volume Two of the Trilogy proposal for a quasi-reorganization of the debt and deficits using GAAP accounting principles and financial statements utilized to move Federal Reserve banking into the US Treasury department and using central banking and crypto our dollar currency for global trade exchange rates.

Finally, the underlying is rebranding America as Americanism based on humanism, replacing all the other isms. Americrats, Meritocracy, Ameritics as the branding for the voters to have a voice in what makes America Great, nothing else. The rest is how to Keep America Great. Ask not what you can do for your party. Ask what you can do for your country to Keep it Great. This is the capital and society working together as a laissez-faire enterprise, to protect a three-party debatable point of view for the constitutional and judicial secure vote to protect our financial and social standing as the United States of America leading peaceful coexistence in a volatile world.

THE AMERICAN ENTERPRISE PARTY
THE TRILOGY VOLUME THREE

AMERICAN WORK ETHIC CHARTER

(a written grant by a sovereign power by which an
institution such as country's work ethic is created and
its rights and privileges are so defined)

Table of Contents

The Trilogy: Peaceful Coexistence with Humanism........................... 1
Charter of Humanism: Restore the American Work Ethic.............. 16
Charter One: Introduction to Building Ethical Behavior 47
Charter Two: Building Character 63
Charter Three: Building Initiative.. 68
Charter Four: Building Security... 73
Charter Five: Building of Lifestyle for Work................................... 83
Charter Six: Building History.. 90
Charter Seven: Building Patriotic Pride 97
Charter Eight: Building Faith and Confidence..............................106
Charter Nine: Building Staying Power 113
Charter Ten: Building Ethical Success..124
Final Word … Laissez Faire … a lifestyle of Work Ethics 167
Author's Bio 183
List of Sources...185
Author's Other Titles...187

The Trilogy, American Peaceful Coexistence with Humanism:

Volume I of the trilogy, tells why we must fight those that idolize and embrace division to conquer the entrepreneurs and enterprising American workers to kill the patriotic spirit of America. The solution is to merge capitalism and socialism into the American Enterprise Party based on peaceful coexistence with Humanism. Why would they be divergent when business combines monetary capital with human capital, in every business, for the successful enterprises that make America Great. The major link to this bloc chain is the capitalist must learn to share for the good of the enterprise and the socialist must learn to show up in and on time, support management and produce a quality product every time. The reinforcement of these principles is the responsibility of constitutional government in a democracy.

In Volume II of the trilogy, tells how to divide and defeat our competition with strength of the enterprise through the synthesis of monetary capital and human capital in trade, finance, quality of life and peaceful coexistence, embodied in the following poem My America the bountiful:

MY AMERICA THE BOUNTIFUL
By Jerry Rhoads published in "The Eighth Wonder of the World"

My America is the feeling of freedom. It's the feeling good when you get up in the morning and can decide what you're going to do that day, who you're going to see, and what you're going to say. It's the feeling that you can make a difference.

It's the feeling you can produce your product, you can sell your produce, and you can benefit from your hard work, unhindered. It's the feeling when you help your children with their homework so they will be able to use their knowledge for growth, for maturity, for the good of the country. It's the feeling when you send them off to school, knowing they will receive a concerned teacher's attention, sensitivity, and guidance.

And knowing as they grow up, they will thrive on their freedom to communicate, to express themselves, to direct their own destiny.

It's the feeling when they graduate from grade school, junior high, and high school that they are taking the steps toward a better life. And when you give their hand away in matrimony, that happiness shall be theirs. For together as husband and wife, they can create the same and even more opportunities for their offspring.

It's that feeling when you can unchain your dog and watch her run free for at least a little while, to watch the expression on her face when she's released from the shackles and the sadness that reappears when she must be chained.

It's the feeling of being in good health, happy with my spouse, with a family as my wealth; as My America is the opportunity to pursue such prosperity unbridled and unfettered.

My America is the freedom of choice to buy the bread I want to buy, to acquire the goods I can afford to acquire, to invest the capital I have saved in ventures I want to take for the love of my family and my country.

My America is being able to communicate in writing, speaking, and in whatever form, language takes, my opinions, my thoughts, my prayers, my visions, and my dreams to those who want to listen and to those enemies of the American way who in themselves have not discovered America.

My America is the blooming rose that has the freedom to grow toward a clear sky and a warm sun, being able to complete its cycle from bloom to plumage to autumn to a dormant grave, only to rise again.

My America is the personal commitment to grab opportunities that will better the country and to set an example for those who follow; what you give must be proportionate to what you take, or the erosion shall remove the sky, the sun, the earth from our grasp.

For in our America and the world resources are limited; the energy, though absolute, is redistributed by our wills. The more astute, the freer we are to create, the better the use of the resources. And left in God's hands, through our America, we create good will, good products, good people, and peace of mind.

My America the bountiful, oh yes, my America, the vision of the poet, the words of the orator, and the minds of the leaders be kind, be patient, be wise, but above all be humble to the reasons and the heritage of our freedom.

Lead us not into temptation, but deliver us from evil ventures and purposes, for thine is mine America, the Kingdom, the power, and the glory, forever.

Amen.

In Volume Three of the trilogy, tells how the science of managing human value for Manology, merges capitalism and socialism as an ideology of Humanism that honors the constitutional values in American enterprise. For those who believe in the value of Humanity as a lifestyle and work ethic towards accepting responsibility to bring America back to embracing all races, genders, religions and creeds in work and lifestyle. To honor history, heroes, the American flag, our constitution, institutions, justice for all, health care for all and God to have a vote for our leaders. Humanitarians who will be accountable for their individual work ethic as a patriot, for the greater good of our great country.

Signed: The American Enterprise Party.

CHARTER TO RESTORE THE AMERICAN WORK ETHIC

"Where Oh Where Has It Gone"
Who Will Do It? Answer Enterprising Americans!

I write about who will do it … hopefully the answer is, it will be by enterprising American workers. But first we must restore worker patriotism that has been destroyed by apathy . . . "Restore the American Work Ethic with Humanism" . . . "Where oh Where has it Gone." It focuses on improving our output by revamping our input of human capital values. Work for the sake of patriotic pride and the quality of life not just for the sake of money and job security. Unfortunately, we the American enterprising workers, are hampered by Big Government and Big Business as being Better and our own ineffectiveness because of a lack of competitiveness and quality as defined by Humanism in a Laissez-Faire free market enterprise.

As for my work ethic I have owned small businesses for 37 years, that I have started from scratch, creating jobs, and envisioning better management systems and methods for principally health care facilities. I have never been unemployed, never drew unemployment or worker's comp and have missed no time from my employment in 59 years.

Patriotically, I have either been extremely lucky or an image of my father a Great common, every day, blue collar, enterprising American who worked in the Firestone Factory in Des Moines, Iowa for 32 years. And even today I remember accompanying my father to union meetings and being influenced as a factory worker myself when I was employed by Firestone one summer. Those images were and are the foundation of the work ethic we seem to have lost and the scenario I propose as the solution to the demise of the American work ethic victim of the new entitlements.

As the author of the American Enterprise Party Platform, I'm a product of a small patriotic farm community in Iowa that was called God's Little Acre in the 1940's as a totally dry town that even frowned on smoking and most certainly did not condone teen pregnancy or divorces. We had no minorities of color or religion . . . we were all poor to almost poor red neck white trash by today's standards. But out of that culture grew a common sense and hard work ethic. My dad for example was never unemployed never drew unemployment, never missed work but went on strike every union contract year, for months on end, to make sure they protected their promised benefits that they never got.

He, at the age of eighteen, and his two brothers had to leave the farm in 1929 during the Great depression when there was no grain for crops and no food for the 8 children, to ride the rails across America . . . his stories about working for a $1 per day with a noon meal, sleeping in hobo camps along the way, drinking moonshine for survival, then returning to the farm when they heard that the depression was over . . . all of these

4

adventures were featured in a recent HBO documentary about the Great Depression of 1929. Making him the man he was . . . a man of work that never swore in his family's presence, never drank in his family's presence, never wanted any management responsibility and never missed work . . . the Iowa work ethic of old.

A HISTORY ON THE RUN

1931 32 33 my dad and his two brothers
Rode the rails during the depression of '29

No food at home
No hope for crops to hone
Boxcar knees
One meal a day please

Cold Coal rail cars
Long barrel shotguns battle scars
Illinoi Central Rock Island Line
No wine and dine

Lonely bums on the run
Cold back of the yards get down son
With warm camp fires
Railroad Dick with a stick that never tires

Trade coal for a meal
Just drunk enough to hide then steal
Earned a dollar per day
If farmer decided to pay

Or given a meal to stay

Hard time served or slave labor
Dirt poor had no money to savor
Life on the rails
Not for gals pals or snails

As hope stops in jails
After hitting the rails
Oh daddy George
It's good that you got home

No longer did you and your brothers have to roam

Dedicated to true patriots of America
George Leonard Rhoads, Wilbur Rhoads, Loren Rhoads
(20, 19 and 18 years old when they did it
Growing older by the hobo minute)

I learned much from him that makes me What and Who I am today and much that I reject as well, including pure socialist, liberal, or Libertarian principles. Is this just conservatism with a different twist . . . no that is not my intent. . . I want more freedom to choose yes, but within the structure of Government of the people, for the people, by the people, not just by me or for me but because of me.

My father once said Firestone management was stupid because they paid union wages for piece work then had their ignorant production control retime the jobs so we made half as much as we used to . . . then we only worked half a day and still made our quotas. He, later on, was promoted to the end of the quality control line, checking steel belted tires for defects. It was when production managers decided to lower the quality standards to reduce the waste and defective tires were pushed through that Firestone was destroyed by lawsuits when the defective tires blew out and Bridgestone, a Japanese company, acquired them. After thirty-four years Dad retired at the age of 64 and sat in his chair for his final 18 years drawing social security and no pension, finally dying in a nursing home at the age of 82. He nor I were ever in the military. He was scheduled to go overseas when the second world war ended and I was a father of four by the age of thirty and exempt from the draft during the Korean and Viet Nam Wars. However, being in cub and boy scouts the first ten years of my life I certainly was indoctrinated with honoring the flag and military veterans. Coming from Iowa it was a given that you stood for the national anthem and recited the pledge of allegiance to the flag and country every scout meeting. I've been a member in Rotary clubs and the Chamber of Commerce for forty years where we performed the same honors every meeting.

My mother was also a depression victim. She lived in a log cabin in Missouri where poverty was rampant due to the depression run on banks and the USA economy. She was a worker and wanted a standard of living that American's workers eventually garnered with free market enterprise. Her father was unemployed and her mother made their clothes and made due with no money. My father and mother, as did millions of all races, migrants and religions, moved to Iowa and the large cities that showed promise. She learned how to sew and made my sister and my clothes while holding down odd jobs in the small town of Indianola. Though my father was a factory worker my mom wanted more than he could provider so she found ways to improve our standard of living creating her own little enterprises.

With my heritage of farmers and factory workers, being an entrepreneur in America and a small business owner myself why would I venture into the buzz saw of conventional wisdom dominated by political pundits who intellectually spout "issues" as facts and facts as "no problems"? Wanting the freedom to choose in the domain of the establishment "Big Brotherhood" Congress, Big Media, the Big Tech, Big Box companies and never putting forth the voice of the silent majority I am willing to put forth solutions to America's decline. Because CNN, Fox News, MSNBC, conservative radio, liberal leanings of the celebrities and universities are not reporting the depth or breadth of America's decline. So, all Americans must standup and demand a third party to remedy the failure of the binary two-party "winner take all" system.

The establishment is in fact the beneficiary of the hard-working enterprising majority who do not have a voice. I, as an unknown, nonintellectual, will be accused of being unqualified politically, negative on America and idealistic on foreign affairs. (Ironically the same rap Donald Trump got when he decided to run for and became the President). Right up front I want to state that America, in my view, is the greatest example of Capital (financial and human) driven Enterprise ever known to man and woman . . . including the Roman and British Empires, the past German and current Chinese versions.

However, all good things come to an end unless there is revitalization of the principles that got us here. So, much of the three volumes of The American Enterprise Party are based on factual data and statistics gleaned over a number of years as I wrote manuscripts regarding the need for political and Government reform to ensure we worship Enterprise rather than institutionalized money. In my research, see the list of sources in Volume II, I found that certain individuals have contributed to contrasting opinions that became movements and did solve social and economic problems. Why? Because they were first of all superior leaders and second dedicated to preserving the honor of our past generations and conserving the future for our children.

Margaret Thatcher and Ronald Reagan were two such leaders of conservatism that inspired me to write this book proposing that we restore old American style Enterprise that evolved out of the slave supported plantations and Aquarian farm communities into the cities of industrial blue-collar workers and profit seeking white collar business owners serving our academic universities and institutions. But now such academic laws and Ph.D. regulators are stifling our effectiveness to utilize what we learn from the Universities and Colleges without allowing the private sector to manage the implementation.

Because of this infringement of Big Institutional Government (Big Brother) on individual creativity and freedom, for the sake of control by the Bigger Box stores, Bigger Technology media and Bigger Universities and Institutions (the Brotherhood), economically called a "Monopsony", (sp … means market controlled by the buyer of last resort … government) we are hampered by our own incompetence because of a lack of competition and quality as defined by free market enterprise. To alter this **"Rome is Burning"** mentality we have to have a balance of the Private Sector and Public Institutions or we will evolve into a world of continued declining initiative and more divorces of thought, marriages and families.

For the sake of the nation's survival as a leader in the world, with China breathing down our necks, the private sector must take an active role under the laws needed to govern moderate and reformative principles of American enterprises by resurrecting the intent of the American Constitution and by erecting a new swing vote political alternative. No longer will the President of the United States and a government of 100 senators, 9 Supreme Court Judges, 435 Congressmen and 22.6 million government employees rule 330 million enterprising Americans without fair representation of enterprising Americans and effective leadership.

Enterprising Americans are workers who defend our country, believe in a greater power, freedom of speech and choice of work, feelings of security in our homes and communities, patriotic to the history and work ethics of the past, willing to take a risk to better their life and country, respect our flag, history and icons of the past, responsible for quality behavior values passed to their children, expect a government that will be accountable for its fiscal affairs and a believer in American democracy, the Republic, our constitution and foreign policies. To this end those who contribute to our America's prosperity shall share in that end. A member in the American Enterprise Party dedicated to a balanced Congress, Presidency and Supreme Court. What is at risk . . . The health and wealth of our nation to be shared, based on individual effort, by all. And just as important retain our great market enterprise leadership as the proof that Democracy works for all races, creeds, religions, genders by a government by the people, of the people for the people.

Why do American's work and pursue a happy life?
1) Optimum standard of living
2) Happy marriage
3) Happy family
4) Security in our homes
5) Safety and civility in our lives

What's the American Dream? Ideals of freedom, equity and opportunity. How is this earned by each individual pursuing that dream?
1) Education in science, technology, engineering and math (Stem).
2) Qualifications including passing grades and recognition of that effort.
3) Life ethics exhibited by values that support the American Dream.
4) Work ethics exhibited by effort towards earning the American Dream.
5) Valued and virtuous performance by our peers and our employers who support civility in the pursuit of the American Dream and its rewards.

Where did these go off track?
1) Identity politics and misdirected government leadership. Bigger is considered better rather than decentralizing the problem solving to those closest to the solution … and term limits for our leaders with accountability analytic reports using generally accepted accounting principles (GAAP) and crime rates as an outcome criterion for each elected official.
2) Tabloid Media inflaming our daily work and lives.
3) Root caused problems treated as issues by our tabloid media and political leadership using fear as an agenda for control of the many by the few.
4) Inequity in pursuing the American Dream that must honor humanism as a priority to stop the erosion of the life and work ethics of the majority.

5) Violence, vulgarity and excess in our entertainment, celebrity and sports salaries and tabloid news taking us away from our civil American values.

6) Deterioration of our inner cities that breed gangs, drugs, prostitution and black on black crime being ignored as a top priority for investment in equity in a quality education, living conditions and small enterprises to serve the underserved citizens. Such injustices cause protests that escalate into destruction of the very neighborhoods that need police protection.

7) Decline in the health and life expectancy of Americans due to the 117 million Americans with at least one chronic medical diagnosis, devastation of the Covid-19 Pandemic and its underlying cost of life and livelihoods of those considered nonessential.

8) The aging of our society led by the Baby Boomers who are retiring at 10,000 per week and filing for Medicare at 7,000 per day. They are not generally healthy having an average 1 to 4 clinical diagnoses as a result of obesity, terminal diseases such as heart failure, cancer, diabetes, etc. Chronic aging is due to unhealthy lifestyles with little exercise, food choices, loss of sleep, divorce, stress from financial problems. As the economy performs so goes the status of the aged. The cost of health care will escalate as the Baby Boomers require critical care then a nursing home.

9) Philosophical Wars of regime change and religious ideologies harmful to peaceful coexistence due to poverty and tyrannical war lords, dictators and cartels using crime as their modus operandi.

How do we get humanism and humanitarian American values back on track? Literally bring the American Dream into American Enterprise where capitalism and socialism work together for enterprising Americans demanding humanism to solve the other isms. By removing the American Nightmare from our lives and work place (get rid of oppressive government, fake tabloid news media, excessive laws and regulations, unsustainable debt, uncivil rights and too many taxes) replacing it with peaceful coexistence.

This requires that the 160 to 200 million enterprising Americans, who work every day, in a civil manner, for the American Dream in their lives and ultimately pay all the bills, have a third- party that represents those values. Where Capitalism plus Socialism equals Humanism in the humanitarian American Enterprise workplace.

A third party, as a swing vote, to represent those ethical life and civil work values in our congress and legislative branch of government. It will bring the right and left extremism to the middle and reimplement government by the people, of the people for the people under God, one nation, indivisible with liberty and justice for all.

In this pursuit we focus our collective energies on civil life values and work ethics that honors our history, forefathers, past leaders, current leaders who pay tribute to the Statue of Liberty and the American Flag. As these symbols make America Great for those immigrants who will legally want the American Dream ... memorialized by citizenship and use of the English language and willingness to pay their way with taxes and investment in our infrastructure. The American Enterprise Party is also a solution to gridlock, uncivil rights and rioting in the streets of America because of social inequities and excessive wealth wasted on wars, riots, violence, vulgarity and unequal pursuit of happiness, good health and prosperity. These are built on the following core values of patriotism, optimism, humanism and the:

- Golden Rule ... treat others with sincerity and respect the way you want to be treated ... honesty is the best trait ... compassion doesn't conflict with right and wrong.
- Pledge of Allegiance to the Flag (with hand over heart optional).
- Stand and sing the National Anthem.
- Prayer in schools as appropriate.
- 1776 Constitutional studies for supporting patriotism and ethics.
- Declaration of Independents studies for freedom and justice.
- Civil Rights and the fourteenth amendment..
- Peaceful coexistence principles involving policing and justice.
- History of 1620 arrival of the Pilgrims on Plymouth Rock, Pennsylvania.

- First amendment rights exercised responsibly.
- Second amendment rights to personal security.
- American history of the Civil War and emancipation of the slaves.
- American history of the World War I and World War II heroes.
- American history of the Civil Rights despite the past wrongs.

LIFE IS A RISK AT BEST

Life revolves around the spindle
Much like the wheel of chance
Looking for some hope to kindle
Smiling as winning numbers become happenstance

Life is so much like the rolling dice
Tumbling to a resting place somehow
And in spite of men and mice
Its meaning rests with an earnest pick and plow

Life is so much like the turning card
We never know what's coming up
Be it smooth or be it marred
You decide how to fill your cup

Life is so much like the bouncing ball
Hitting and missing the slots you want
Awaiting the right chance to call
But you're the author of the plot

Life is much like the numbers turning
The odds are not always in your favor
Unless you find a worthwhile yearning
And good intentions to savor

Life is s much like the Bacharach box
Holding the secrets fast inside

Not easily or freely releasing the locks
Forcing you to develop a hard-earned pride

Life is a risk at best
Nothing good comes with a guarantee
So no matter how hard you guessed
You'll never be a winner until you decree

That life is more much more than
To gamble away
Each day just being free to lose your pay
Your way

Waiting for a giveaway
When enterprise makes your day

USA is the only pure democracy since Rome and the American Enterprise Party is the only way to merge capitalism and socialism into an enterprising society of humanism sharing of the wealth based on effort, intelligence and producing better jobs, better wages and better lives. Where tribes are converted into productive teams with goals to learn then earn income from outcome. We all have been given life for free but love of life has to be earned. Since real life isn't pure objectivity or subjectivity there are certain principles that embrace both:

1. Human nature requires rationality for individual reasoning and feelings to be valued in a free marketplace.

2. Free market is a continuum to ever create. Free market capitalism is the social subjective view of objective value.

3. Government interference creates inflation, unemployment, gridlock, debt and deficits.

4. Economic control by the benevolent producers not the arbitrary enforcers is the essence of a democracy.

5. Capitalism must share in the profits of economic sacrifice and surplus of effort.

6. Socialism must share in the responsibility of producing quality, profitable and value-based outcomes by free individuals valued in proportion to their ethics and effort.

7. Intelligence applied as Humanism and peaceful coexistence is for survival of democracy.

8. Capitalism plus socialism resulting in better jobs, better wages, better lives while pursuing individual good.

CHARTER OF HUMANISM

Restore the American Work Ethic
(Bring back Systemic Humanism)
(Where Oh Where Has It Gone)

H oly
U nto
M an
A nd
N eed
I denity
T o
Y ield peace

"When you work you are a flute through whose heart the whispering of the hours turns to music . . . and what is it to work with love? It is to weave the cloth with threads drawn from your heart, even as if your beloved were to wear that cloth." –Kahlil Gibran, *The Prophet*

W illfull
O wnership
R enders America
K ing of the mountain

E ffort
T ied and
H eld
I nto a
C onstitution

Ethic, defined as a set of moral principles, esp. ones relating to or affirming a specified group, culture, or form of conduct: "the puritan ethic". As proposed in the first two volumes we need to practice the principles of Humanism. It is the humanitarian worker who shows up on time, is diligent on the job and goes the extra mile in serving his/her employer. Believes in human rights and has a human survival instinct. Which is tolerance, compassion, patience, truthfulness and sense of value.

The golden rule "those with the gold shall rule" to be replaced by
"Those with common sense have the humankind votes to rule"
The rest are billy goats spouting racism, socialism, capitalism,
fascism, wokeism, ism ism ism when all we want is humanism"

THE CULTURE OF HUMANISM

The complexities of our world
The battles for flags unfurled
Is there simplicity there
That can explain

How to have happiness in spite of pain

Is it so hard to know
Not why but how to grow
Does it have to be deciphered
By the professors of Harvard and Yale
Turning the glow of life
To a confused pale

Why does it have to be so hard
Why is it scientific to have grass in the yard
Or success dependent upon the turning of a card
Nay that's only the human's way
Wanting to impress
To assume the power
And control the press

Rather than giving a simple yes
We pull it through the cloak of complexity
Watering it down with ingenuity

17

Until there's no such thing as purity
No such thing as the ease of an understandable truth
And the uncast shadow of youth

That merely assumes that we have to live through monsoons
And shouldn't have to control the weather
Or recreate the aerobics of a feather
It's not necessary to multiply divide and carry
For the sake of making it hard
Till jokers are wild holding the hole card

With common sense, virtue and good will
Lost to the complexity of nonsense and hell
While the soothsayers spout
And the pseudo intellectuals pout
About
Politics climate change terrorists
And all other indefinable events

By referring everything to an algorithm
Or an Evangelical hymn
To make sure once again
That a Trump card doesn't win

Where the other cards in the deck
Are dumbing down the electorate
Making transparency after they inspect
And keeping public opinion in check
Saying ... "Now look"
"Free health care is a right"
"It's an Issue not a problem"
"Now Listen here"
"It's God's will"
"Right to life"
"Right to choose"
"Black lives matter'
"White lives matter more"
"Prayer out of the schools"
"Debate away the country's fate"

"Free college tuition"
"Unlimited minimum wage"
"Maximum wage"
"Public officials are above reproach"
"The President's lying"
"It's a political media's fault"
"Fake news is singing the blues"

"Where a problem is called and issue"
"Issue issue get me a tissue"
While the ACLU says "let the flag burn and
There's no such thing as straight or fag"

What happened to common everyday
Horse sense
Gambled away
On dollars and nonsense
Oh for the forties and fifties when a dollar was gold
And patriotism never grew old

Purchasing votes with good ole common cents
Instead of debt, bit coins and finger prints
Doing away with all those isms
With the chartered principles of Humanism

BLM wants reparation
ANTIFA wants War
Marxists want cancel culture
While humanism wants peaceful resolution
(Reason minus revolution = resolution)
With life liberty and civil pursuit of opportunism
Without bias for racism, socialism, capitalism,
Wokeism, ism, ism, ism is ...

A nonviolent humanitarian culture
of love, virtue and peaceful coexistence
Called Pe American Dream of Humanism for Humankind

THE CHARTER: *the American enterprise Party does herewith represent*
nonviolent humanitarian culture of love, virtue and peaceful coexistence

called the American Dream of Humanism for Humankind. Where all Human Lives Matter.

Li Hongzhi, Chinese founder of Falun Gong writes "Pacify the External by Cultivating the Internal. If the population values self-cultivation and the nurturing of virtues, and if both officials and civilians alike exercise self-restraint in their minds, the whole nation will be stable and supported by the people. Being solid and stable, the nation will naturally intimidate foreign enemies and peace will thus reign under heaven". Li Hongzhi a sage and leader of the Falun Gong movement of 350 million Chinese who have opted out of Chinese Communist Party. Quoted from the Epoch Times, June 2021.

Jerry Rhoads author: *The essence of this movement is to divide and conquer communism with humanism. To quote Confucius the Chinese prophet "the man who chases two rabbits catches neither. And Michelangelo: genius is eternal patience for excellence.*

HLM is Human lives matter.

HLM wants resolution
BLM wants reparation
ANTIFA wants revolution

Marist slogan "production for people not profit"
Marxists will dehumanize to cancel our risk culture
While humanism wants "peaceful resolution for profit"
(Reason minus racist revolution = resolution)
With life liberty and civil pursuit of opportunism
Without bias for racism, socialism, capitalism,
Wokeism, ism, ism, ism is …

THE CHARTER: *America is also the land of free laissez faire. Where promises made are promises kept revolving around Human values of peaceful coexistence for profit. Then profit can only exist to the extent it fulfills human needs and the wants so governed by the people, for the people, of the people under our constitution and declaration of independence.*

Is America the land of laissez faire not lazy faire?
Yes, where the Any Rand objective monetary capital marries the subjective Peter Drucker Human capital, it gestates the great American Enterprise to create patriotic humanism ... as effective subjects manage themselves within the team objectives. Pus, management by objectives becomes management of subjective.

Patriotism is the love of an individual for his or her country. Nationalism a theory that seeks to establish a world of free and independent nations. Neither requires or subjects nations or individual's subordination to a shared universal law but work ethics do. This allows individual patriots personal reasons to work for individual humanism not just for the greater good. Such as China, North Korea and Russia demanding loyalty to the motherland. Setting the common good as dependent on the supreme elite rule of law. Then proletariat is patriotic to the Politburo for whom they work.

Those of progressive zeitgeist socialist theory would look to government to be the purchaser of last resort and giver of all security and safety for the greater good. I would term this the "Big Brother Dream" for the Brotherhood and its workers. The individual is no longer the focus of life, liberty and the rules of law ... love and personal achievement is deemed offensive because it takes from others to be attained. A true evolving dystopia envisioned by Orwell's 1984, where hate overruled Love.

The American Enterprise Humanistic Work Ethic is to combat the Progressive Woke Government Edicts for Human Behavior. As is "The Brave New World" of genetic mutations and synthetic viruses. With Big Brother and the Brotherhood standing for a culture where war is peace, slavery is freedom and ignorance is strength. AKA Orwellian dystopia.

The American Humanism Dream (Camelot utopia) on the other hand is built on **capital infusion** and the **human assets'** work ethic. "The will to work" in a free market is inherited from our patriotic forefathers and must be sustained by each of us. The willful ownership by rendering effort to be a king of the mountain has motivated enterprising workers since the first revolution in 1776 (not 1619 a year before the pilgrim settlers arrived in 1620). Since then, we have allowed our government regulators to impose restrictions and minimum standards on the growth of the private sector using taxation at forty-six different levels to control businesses while building institutional government at all levels. Including our public education system that is threatening to rewrite our history with critical race theory to the rejection of patriotic American families. Such thinking is reverse racism by thinking in squares not "let freedom ring" … our constitution specifically defines patriotic America and Americans' work ethic not needing a reinterpretation due to a hate crime in Minneapolis.

Those protesters who want to deify George Floyd are squarely wrong … to make the world go round clearly, we need to fix our system of justice and will be a given with the election of a third-party candidate as the swing vote … But a black revolution based on a series of events that justify riots is a revolt against our American Dream, which is color blind, under our constitution … To those who are color bound forget our legacy, it is a revolt against peaceful coexistence, that will fail. To this we enterprising Americans must pledge our patriotism and work ethic to change our inner cities and underprivileged communities into enterprise zones and provide Charter education and rehabilitation of our ghettos and slums into opportunity zones for supporting color blind small business enterprises.

This must, by taking away all excuses of the progressives, illicit the support and labor of the 30,000 gangs with over a million gun slinging members in America, for rebuilding their hoods into examples of the best of the Green New Deal, as amended, to make America equal and equitable in its application of the American Dream… that means equality is personal freedom, equity means the resources to restore and reimagine our inner cities and small marginalized communities into productive powerhouses serving a worldwide underprivileged market. Then we are more capable of competing with China that has 748 million workers and other emerging economies in a rational and accountable enterprise.

Because, as a "winner take all" two-party system gridlocked 50/50 Congress where there is no consensus to focus on national problem solving. As established in Volume One an effective third party, acting as the swing vote, will instill equity into our constitutional system of government and prevent a binary two-party failure of gridlock and ineffective rulemaking.

With the consumer price index rising from a $1 worth of purchasing power in 1955 to requiring 10.58 times as much to stay up with costs in 2021 and the unemployment rate floating between 4.1 percent in 1955 to 10.8% in 1982 to 40% in 2020 during the Pandemic. It is no wonder that the decline in the American life value and work ethic prevents businesses from creating more high-quality jobs. As prices increase due to the cost of capital (interest rates being gamed by the Federal Reserve system) and the reduction of purchasing power of the dollar, revenues, profits and capital will spiral downward and the national debt upward. Our financial condition is woefully built on a "House of Cards" and a Senate of Shards, by not reporting on generally accepted accounting principles (GAAP) demonstrated on the national debt clock www.usdebtclock.org.

It is the new entitlements that deprive enterprise of much-needed capital to create jobs and reduce American workers' dependency on government. It is unemployment benefits, minimum wage, public service pension debt, stimulus bribes to not work, workers' compensation, food stamps, welfare, reparation, enforcement agencies for collecting taxes, that are utilizing our depleted tax revenues. Some one hundred fifteen million public-sector workers in the United States—including teachers, police and firefighters, state and municipal employees, judges, and legislators—and another seven million federal and military employees participate in government pension plans. These pension systems are extraordinarily diverse in design, investment policy, and governance, and they face substantial challenges as the government-sector workforce ages and governments are asked to take on new and different tasks. "This is in itself will sink our future".

Are the public-service pension fund managers (i.e., California Teachers Association Pension Fund) investing in wind energy or green proposal or in the American economy or funding wars or the development of weapons of mass destruction or promoting the intrusion of labor unions on capital deployment? The point is there is no accountability in the funding of or the use of these resources other than complex budget proposals that state and local legislative branches choose to pass or put in abeyance until the electorate forgets about it.

For example, opening the borders to migrant workers, one come all, or closing down the Keystone Pipeline laying off 15,000 workers or condoning rioters and defunding the police or accepting that it is permissible to have 300 million guns in circulation or letting our inner cities be crumbling and giving rise to 30,000 gangs embedded in our society as drug cartel employees. All of this is impacting the creation of clean energy jobs that then affects the American eroding work ethic and humanitarian lifestyles. All I can say is God Save America from itself.

GIVE ME MY RIGHTS

I am born to be free of tyranny and a monarchy

I was born on Thanksgiving Day
Baptized on Christmas Day
Raised in a free country somewhat stable
And given the opportunities available

To each sunrise I rose
And as soon as I could stand up and walk
I began chasing whatever I chose
Taking responsibility for what I stalk

And if I play seek and find
I couldn't really blame another
Not even my dad or mother
It was I who chose where I resigned

For it was up to me
I really didn't contemplate or tout
That making the most of being free
Is putting my hand out

Or expecting equality from the State
I could stand on my own two feet
Taking care of myself was my family's fate
And the bills I had to meet

Yes freedom to me was an opportunity
But I guess I'm "out of sorts"
Not understanding the system of torts
Nor the courts as a handout of immunity

For they seem to be stating some deed
And protection under the law
About freedoms guaranteed
That "kind of hang up" in my craw

For Democracy is not a guarantee
Of freedom, equity or equality
It's merely an opportunity for you and me
And those who choose and demand to be free

Most likely some lives are the pits
Though they may lose from their toils
Or are the pathetic hypocrites
Upon which pity spoils

Even though they can climb up on their back legs
With hands out and a lowly soul that begs
I must implore them for what they are
With their hand in someone else's cookie jar

Barking and begging on their back legs
They're saying I demand equity in terms of equality
I've got the right for my country's free
And it's "tis of thee" opportunity

Though we're supposed to have democracy
Guaranteeing everything to me
So give me my rights to this I demand
And to that to which I stand

Here in this dissolving quick sand
Of patricians under a flag of the red blue and whites
Impairing America's ability to demand
That all living here have to earn their rights

To this Plato understood
Unto which democracy stood
"Where even dogs would want to be free
Standing on their hind legs demanding equality"

And they're never going to be free
Because it takes an acquiring mind to pursue opportunity
In our land of "tis of thee"
Not just for you or me

In a troubled world where all lives matter
America is what it is due to diversity
Inclusive we must stand together
That's being equitably and equally free

An opportunity for you and me

My Story of 175+175+175 = Failure

At a skilled nursing facility, I took on, which was decertified and called "Death Valley" by the surveyors, there were 207 beds with plummeting occupancy. It had 175 patients that did not want to be there, 175 families who did not want to come there, and 175 employees who did not want to work there—quite a big undertaking to turn failure into winning a Super Bowl.

Within five days of taking over without even an administrator's license, a ninety-three-year-old contracted patient drowned in the whirlpool while a foreign therapist charted behind a privacy screen. The next day I was on TV trying to explain the accident, which the attorney general called neglect and criminal abuse.

My attitude of "I am going to fix this mess" and a forgiving family got me through to the next big problem. Actually, after that and for the next six months it got worse: 200 percent turnover, 25 percent absenteeism, 50 percent absenteeism on weekends, theft of patients' valuables, air conditioning that broke down for two weeks. Surveyors were there every day with their humidity and temperature thermometers, just waiting to shut us down.

My staff was made up of legal or illegal immigrants who weren't properly trained nor effective but wanted what I wanted. More respect, more pride and a bigger paycheck. I had Polish bed makers, Mexican housekeepers, Filipino LPNs, East Indian night staff, Black American CNAs, white RNs, Hispanic dietary staff, many of whom were probably not legal aliens. Not a team, but a group of workers focused on paychecks and their departments, not on the patients. I found out that I didn't have the quick fix and probably made things worse by doing nothing but reacting to family, patient, staff complaints.

Even an ineffective leader sometimes does nothing and becomes a leader. During a snowstorm that November, only half the staff showed up for work and for seventy-two hours the facility ran better without troublemakers and thieves. Per my phone instructions to the Assistant Director of Nursing, the staff needed to team up and focus on priorities assigned by her. When I got there, the ADON and lead aide had organized the staff into teams and were performing as they never had before. Priorities were done first and busywork was shelved. After the snowstorm, I had an epiphany as it dawned on me that before the storm all of the staff only worked half a day; and after, half the staff got more done in a day than they did in a week before. Quite an eye-opener, so much so I decided we were not going back to the old ineffective departmental structure but were going to stay with the teams set up in my absence. The rest is history.

In conclusion, this epiphany changed my view of the infrastructure of nursing homes. As teams only focused on the patients' priority problems and organized to implement the care plan interventions, we achieved efficiency and effectiveness never before attained. Productivity was based on outcomes we could get reimbursed for and quality was a byproduct of our control of the processes. By our next QUIP (quality incentive payment) and annual survey we were recertified and received a clean survey with five of the six stars of quality awarded exemplary providers, which meant more money for better quality.

The byword for this miracle I experienced, is taking a staff with no purpose and turning it into a team with a purpose is Enterprise. My realization that our staff was handcuffed to antiquated management awoke with the snowstorm. From that day on I implemented "learn to earn and skill to bill" programs to provide each staff member a career path to their American Dream. This was built on the program I learned at Arthur Andersen & Co. Each person was the center of their life's aspirations and goals. All I had to do, as their leader, was to activate them in an organization of winning not losing to their job performance.

In other words, doing their jobs with excellence and effort as their goal we all were winners … and in the process the patients received quality of care and improvement of their lives. Out of this grew my pay for performance program based on "skill to bill and learn to earn" career plans that evolved into the so called "Death Valley" environment being replaced by a six-star facility that was the envy of our competition and the joy of our patients and their families.

Unfortunately, this could not last forever because the facility was sold and I was replaced as the Administrator by a chain operator who reversed all of the changes, we had accomplished to save money and the facility was returned to a warehouse for the elderly, not a care house for restored patients so they could return home or to the community. My staff was devastated and thought the new owners were crazy for firing the coach taking them to the Super Bowl (their words at my departure party where they gave me a trophy for believing in them).

Out of this experience comes my educated opinion:

(Another epiphany I had was to pay the performing employees (See Exhibit D in Volume II) on service excellence. Why not pay fewer efficient staff more for providing quality work, rather than more staff less for whatever they decide to do or not do?)

At the root cause of the quality problem is the current regulatory minimum standards and minimum wage that promotes mediocrity by using them to penalize the employers for mismanagement of the human resources. Using the work ethic formula for a civil productive life we can teach workers to fish not just give them fish where more is never enough. When more is enough then it's from a productive work ethic not a give-a-way entitlement.

My Fox Valley Story Ending of 179+200+200 = Success

From April 1987 to July 1989 the 175+175+175 failure of 175 workers who didn't want to work there, 175 Patients that didn't want to be there and 175 families that wouldn't come there to visit was changed in one year to 179 workers who wanted to work there, 200 patients who liked living there and 200 families who came to visit their loved ones. Why were there only 179 workers when you left? ... we were able to do more for more patients with less staff ... to me that is the biggest success of the Enterprise Model of care we instituted. My next stop in August 1989 was to Carington living Center in Glendale Heights, Illinois ... another 175+175+175 = failure that become the same 175+200+200 = success by September 1991. From there I went from contract management to consulting with 140 more skilled nursing facilities until September 4, 2009 when my wife, son and I purchased three skilled nursing facilities and sold them in July 2012 and June 30, 2015 after converting

them to the Enterprise Model of care. All this is documented in my health care books listed in the back of this book. In Volume II there is a brief summary of why we sold them.

Work Ethic: A Formula for an Honest and Productive Life as the first step to Wisdom and Success

A Culture of Ethical Behavior . . . Is it the—

- Best Worker . . . focused on the job at hand with the discipline to pursue completion and accept responsibility for outcome.
- Best Employee . . . honest and reliable when the chips are on the table without fear of complications.
- Best Person . . . takes responsibility for others over the job and will take the fall for others if justified.
- Best Technician . . . left brain intelligent when there is a pattern to follow and documents work.
- Best Theorist . . . looks for an easier path to completion with no preconceived notion on results.
- Best Tactician . . . rote in setting up the work flow with efficiency and productivity as priorities.
- Best Strategist . . . visionary, a planner and a self-starter that moves beyond assignments.
- Best visionary . . . positive work ethic and most creative, less worried about risks and obstacles, will change the world.
- Best Bureaucrat . . . more disciplined, though empathic towards the private sector and communicates rules objectively.
- Best Entrepreneur . . . resistive to instructions, wants to travel a new path and excels at problem solving pursuing outcomes for earning income.
- Best Religion … teaching virtues with values rather than preaching issues.
- Best Human … being kind and positive about diversity that is color blind to black and white superiority.

Workers are first employees with certain of the above talents and functions but ethics are a learned habit taught and enforced by ethical leaders. So, each position must honor a culture of virtuous ethics practiced by its leadership's values. In an environment where outcome means income for every worker.

Again, Adam Smith's insight gives us clarity.
"We are more industrious than our forefathers, because in the present times, the funds destined for the maintenance of industry are much greater in proportion to those that are likely to be employed in the maintenance of idleness. Our ancestors were idle for want of sufficient encouragement to industry. It is better, says the proverb, to play for nothing than work for nothing. In mercantile and manufacturing towns where the inferior ranks of people are chiefly maintained by the employment of capital, they are, in general, industrious, sober, and thriving".

The mind feasts on the bad luck of others to feel good about its own fear of failure.

It is the thought that is ethical, not the act; the act is purely a response to thinking honestly and responsibly.

How can we think ethically and work respectfully? Did Jesus think ethically? Did Martin Luther King live ethically? Of course, the answer is yes, but how did they form that way of thinking? Was it a birthright or life just, right? To get it just right we all have to think right and live right as the "what," the effort to do so is the "how," and the "when" is now and forever.

Today's thinking builds tomorrow's ethic, tomorrow's ethics builds your life. Be it work or success, each of us must create it. That is the ethic of meaningful work.

Entrepreneurs are the backbone of the economy of a flourishing country because they are responsible for initiating new businesses which are extremely helpful in the acceptance of economic risk and creating financial reward.

However, work ethics in American enterprise is losing ground. Why? . . . Because there is no active representation of self-worth. The Democrats promise government worth and the Republicans promise business wealth. But who represents personal enterprise worth? The American worker is the most enterprising in the world, but that value is declining. Why? Big Brother government and personal wealth of a few in the Brotherhood stifles the growth of the many.

What is needed to reverse this social and economic backsliding? Another political and great enterprise point of view must emerge based on the following ethical platform:

1. Work and humanity ethic must be nurtured by improving on the known or invent better.
2. Education must focus on American history, creativity and risk taking as a culture (it takes both human and behavioral science).
3. Government must serve, not sever, creation of work and the humanity ethic and human relationships around in a peaceful coexistent world.
4. The wealthy must reinvest their profits and capital in American small businesses and the work and humanity ethic they represent.
5. Humanism with its humanitarian virtues must fill the void between Capitalism and Socialism.
6. Capitalism is objective view of profits as monetary value. Socialism is the subjective view of human capital.
8. Socialism is the subjective pursuit of profit as economic value based on supply and demand from self-interest and production.

The four planks of this platform will require a reconstitution of our society based on former values:

*   Life is the vehicle for virtuous humanism
*   Liberty is the fuel for patriotism
*   Pursuit of happiness is the engine for equity with optimism

- Work is the creator of all human value for equality and equity in a positive environment.
- Enterprise is the freedom of each enterprising individual to succeed for country and oneself (ask not what your company can do for you but what you can do for the company ... paraphrased from JFK).

Humanitarian leaders must deal with solving social and ethical problems, not just debating their personal biases and differences of opinion (so-called issues) such as:

- America's focus on race rather than equity and peaceful coexistence (the black revolution is in process when protests turn into riots, stealing and destruction). It is time to put that passion, as opportunity zones, to work to clean up our ghettos and slums that are criminal zones.
- America's health decline due to chronic disease and Pandemics (Life expectancy down for the first time in history. Our current health care is driven by treatment not prevention and preservation). Prescription drugs aren't an outcome but a source of provider and street gangs income.
- America's self-value decline (Underprivileged student education graduation rate as less than 30%).
- America's peaceful actions decline due to Crime rate (300 million guns and 30,000 gangs, with over a a million criminals employed by cartels and mafia).
- America's net worth declines in GDP and GNP, due to debt and deficits wasting resources (national credit rating at an all-time low).
- America's resolve declines due to loss of faith in our markets (Dow Jones Stock Market Score and imbalance of trade are a derivative bubble set to burst with the debt, deficits, Pandemic bringing inflation and asset devaluation with them).
- America's happiness decline (2.4 million divorces and 47,000 suicides in America each year).

- American Dream pursued by immigrants from all over the world flooding our streets and institutions (homeless and drug cartels embedding a migrant sales force that's infecting our cities). Employment of mind and body is the passion we need for instilling the work ethic in every American's life.
- America, when growth of the nation stops, decay within begins. The science of self-health of the person and the nation is at stake.

> **S** cience
> **E** ngineered
> **L** ife
> **F** ulfillment
>
> **H** ow you think determines your fate
> **E** thics determine your destination
> **A** ction determines your journey
> **L** ife determines your legacy
> **T** ime productively expended
> determines your ethics and rewards
> **H** ealth is a journey not a destination

Healthy body, mind, heart, soul = self-health HABITS

The Pandemic of 2019, 20 and 21 highlights the need for an ounce of prevention and vaccines that protect us from a weakened immunity to future viruses. Currently in the USA there are 117 million people with one of more chronic illnesses, 1.6 million in nursing homes and 77 million baby boomers with 10,000 filing for social security every month and 7,000 filing for Medicare every week. This includes 100 million who are considered obese with the leading annual cause of death: 647457 heart disease, 599,108 cancer, 160,201 chronic lower respiratory disease, 146,383 stroke and 83,564 diabetes, plus 559,000 due to covid-19 and 550,000 per year in nursing homes (50% due to the flu and pneumonia). That totals 180 million Americans out of 330 million that are at risk for future viruses due to weakened immunity. They and the remainder must pursue remedies beyond inoculation and prescription drugs with better lifestyles, habits, food choices and exercise activities.

Also, American workers are enterprising but work brittle. The five-day, forty hours per week, 180 hours per month, 2,080 hours per year are in the past. Working at being an American is a twenty-four-hour per day proposition. Until the private sector takes back control of the biggest enterprise in the world (the American economy) the public sector will stifle creativity for the sake of lawmaking, regulatory intrusion and job-breaking. With physical and mental health an afterthought.

INDIVIDUALS COUNT

In America people are independent
Due to a Declaration in 1776
Due to the Constitution in 1774
Due to the Civil Rights Act of 1964
Due to World Wars I and II
Due to the First and Second Amendments

So why do we feel inhibited by Government
Is Enterprise really Free
Since each American is an Enterprise
And most laws are to inhibit this dynamic
(With 40,000 bills proposed and 5,000 laws passed each year)
By lawmakers who vote their own agenda

Not ours any more

What exactly is ours
Is it our work
Is it our ambition
Is it our dreams
Is it our responsibilities
Is it our FREEDOM to vote

Then why do we feel helpless
It is not our authority
It is not our preference
It is not our risk that counts
It is not our decision to go to war
It is not our opinion on peace
Not now
Freedom is a right Freedom is a necessity
Freedom is our only weapon
Against power and poverty
Against enforcement
Against Tyranny

Will Americans let go of freedom
Will Americans go down peacefully
Will Americans lose independence
Ask yourself if you want 40,000 laws per year
Ask yourself if you want lawmakers endlessly making laws
Ask yourself if you have given up or will stand up
For your independence and freedom that won't wait
Your individual ethics collectively will determine America's fate

BE THE RIDER

What do you want to be?

Avoiding sharp turns and personal burns
Are what the real you can handle
As challenges not concerns
Being the rider not the saddle

It's what you're all about
So don't tell me you just want to be you
And then ask me who you should be
For you've never learned to be yourself

Is this incrimination or discrimination
No it's the mountain we all climb
Mount Everest of life
Meant to be hard and not sublime

There's no giving into the pursuit
Nothing can be easier
Then a slide in an avalanche
Of rejection and deflection

Stand up ride that wave
To the highest summit
It's your life you save
And avoid the plummet

Avoiding sharp turns and personal burns
Are what the real you can handle
As challenges not concerns
Being the rider not the saddle

Mounted on someone else's mantel
Or buried in a pauper's chattel
Due to bad choices
And critics voices

W illfull
O wnership
R enders America
K ing of the mountain

E xercise your
T hought and
H ealth
I nto job
C reation

THEN YOU'RE THE RIDER NOT THE SADDLE

PARITY OR DIVERSITY

*Parity is "The state or condition of being equal
especially regarding status or pay" Diversity is"
any dimension that can be used to differentiate groups
and individuals from one another.*

*The creation of man
Yea is it to equality
Or yea is it to opportunity
Is man created equal
Or were they created <u>to be</u> equal*

*Even babies are different
In size in color in personality
So why does this make us equal
At birth and till we die*

*We aren't and never will be equal
Equal rights and opportunity
Not hands tying
For lack of trying*

*Is parity a democracy or a social ideology
Do the scales need to be balanced or are they fair
When in balance with nature
And when in receipt of effort
The scales tip to those who put forth
And tip the scales their way*

*Parity a road to equality
Or the epitaph of dichotomy
Only the perceptive shall see*

And only the seeing shall perceive
That even time favors the purveyor of the work
That even heaven beckons those who shall not shirk
Their duties and good graces is their advent
Through industry health and good judgment

Yes it tis the purpose for clarity
To define and expose parity
As the Satan of society
As the downfall of Houdini
And the ego of Mussolini
Give us parity

Or give us give us give us give us
But in all sincerity
Only the doers shall believe
Only the unlike shall conceive
And the successes achieve
Only the humble shall receive

If parity is only a means to deceive
And

Then the pursuit of Equality and Equity is through Diversity and Inclusion, defined as the achievement of a work environment in which all individuals are treated fairly and respectfully, have equal access to opportunities and resources to contribute fully to the organization's profitable success.

In my opinion the greatest inventions of mankind are:

1. The printing press and the bible.
2. The assembly line invented by Ford Motor company.
3. The Wright Brothers discovery of flight by humans.
4. The World War II patriotic, diverse work force of women and a military of men winning the war in four years over evil and tyranny.

5. The computer, the internet and cell phones.
6. The wedding of monetary capital and human capital into an enterprise.
7. Democracy and the American constitution the platform for enterprise.
8. But the most dynamic was the concept of the many to one teamwork.

   a. Such as Iwo Jima, Omaha Beach, 9/11, the Olympiad, 1776 Declaration of Independence, 1492 discovery of America, 1620 the colonists and pioneers' discoveries coast to coast and team sports.

   b. Humanism built on patriotic work ethic and peaceful coexistence in a world of diversity of color, religion, gender, creed and personal aspirations.

Being an Iowan by birth and Chicagoan by trade, my favorites teams, of course are the Bears and the Cubs because perennial losers become winners based on the many becoming one. Mike Ditka led the Bears to an eventual Super Bowel based on a team of diverse individuals who were told that he was going to the Super Bowl and anyone that didn't believe that was not going to make his team. Chicago hadn't had a winner since 1964 when George Halas did the same thing … inspiring the individuals to act as one to become Super Bowl champs in 1985. They haven't done it since.

On the other hand, the Chicago Cubs had never won the World Series in 108 years of trying. Along came Brian Epstein who had led the Boston Red Sox to their first World Series in 84 years and the Rickets family the new owners. Previously, the Cubs were owned by the Wrigley chewing gum family then the Chicago Tribune newspaper people. Mr. Epstein brought the new concept in baseball called analytics wedded to talent, to Chicago, after its discovery by the Oakland Athletics under "Money Ball" great, Billy Beane. Who, as general manager, took a loser to a 22-game winning streak, the most in major league history, but fell short in the World Series. This, along with hiring an inspirational leader in Joe Madden to pull the talent together, the Cubs forged the 2016

World Series winner … the only one in the Cubs history. None since or maybe ever.

As for my Fox Valley and Carrington teams … we were perennial losers until the snow storm and my 175 diverse many team members became one to form a championship team that won six stars of quality from the Illinois surveyors' QUIP (quality incentive program) challenge … a rag tag group that didn't know what a star was let alone the six stars we won by becoming the best we could be.

My long-winded point here is the same taught by every coach in sports and life that the individual standing alone is weak compared to the individuals working together for a common purpose. That's the Olympiad, the greatest invention by man and women of all colors, creeds, religions, genders and political parties. **It brings the many to one purpose … winning the biggest championship of all time for their country… Global Humanism and peaceful coexistence of our diverse and dynamic world called the Good Earth. Based on …**

W illful
O lympians
R ender America
K ing of the mountain

E xercise their
T raining for
H umanity
I nto gold medal
C reation

THE OLYMPIAD

Is where the world is at peace
A goal they accomplish
Olympians prepare for a day to not cease
Pursuing their dreams and wish

If not victory's thrill
But the agony of defeat
It's an honor still
For they can always repeat

As a challenge each four years
Athletes compete
With smiles and tears
Making the earth complete

While the riders boaters rowers and runners
Outrun the hare
The gymnasts dancers and horses are stunners
Nothing can compare

The swimmers synchronized and diverse chase
The bands and hands on a clock
Beating others in place
Getting off the board and block

Weight lifters and boxers grunt
Having built strength with a bicep curled
Upon their shoulder's as a stunt
Hoisting the weight of the world

Volley ball and field hockey are next on the agenda
Whether in the sand or the gym

Their reaction will send and defend
Sensation past the extended limb

Golf is back on the role
Powering the small ball
Towards that shrinking hole
Coercing the competitors as they fall

Baskets and hands are for carrying
While handballs and basketballs are for playing
Put them together pairing
A game for scoring each gaming swing

Tennis badminton and table tennis
Aren't just a birdie or ping pong
They're the fastest sports as a menace
To the Aussies Asians and American throng

Baseball is resurrected
A national sport made worldwide
With the Olympics interjected
For gold to take home the pride

Football rugby and now (futbol) ball is no longer
Just an American obsession
It's Worldwide soccer that's stronger
Then any super bowl sensation

Shooting archery and boating are popular
For the finer part of the heart
Taking us to the spectacular
We don't usually impart

Wrestling taekwondo and jujitsu are for the fit
Muscles and determination

Squeezed into a singlet
Make for a great exhibition

Fencing trampoline and water polo
Gives the diversity to be gamed
The team sport and the solo
Presents scores to be tamed

Running triathlon and speed walking a natural chase
Creating a perfect pairing
Of endurance and staying on pace
While the fans are left staring

Cycling and a Marathon race
Are the contests for the best
Endurance and the long-distance pace
With small countries taking on the test

Pole vaulting and the Fosbury flop
Challenge gravity
While sprinters and milers stop
When the winners take a knee

Broad jumping stepping or skipping
Defies imagination
Flying through the thin air then dipping
To bring a medal to their nation

Throwing a heavy steel ball or throwing
A disc or a spear
Are no longer just showing
That mankind has no peer

As the finale of track and field
Is the pentathlon and the decathlon

44

Nothing will or can yield
But the setting sun

Where the many are now one

Our champions and heroes
Compete worldwide
From Beijing to those
Exotic places expressing their pride

All this makes for the national
Counting of the medals
But it's more rational
If we count the friendships, it peddles

The Olympiad the medals stand
Playing the national anthems
Allows us to know and understand
How worldwide peace redeems

It defeats terrorism fascism communism
That are based on fear
By being the fusion
Of all mankind from afar every fourth year

Competing not for rules but for
Principles held dear
200 countries thus opening the door
Where the athletes' bonding is clear without fear

Leading to Humanism as peaceful coexistence commences
As the solution to political wars and religious indifferences

Charter One

Introduction to Work and Longevity—
Building Ethical Behavior

P rofit

R ules

O ur

F inancial

I nterests and

T axes

Profits are defined as the return on invested capital through human capital work products. But our self-health research found that work is the lifeblood of profit and longevity because it keeps the brain and organs stimulated with energizing blood flow, while inactivity destroys brain cells and synopses and the will to live.

At the same time, the political consultants say "don't try to educate the voter, let them blindly follow the money-tics, and not think they can tell you what to do". The other factor, of "why we have to do it", is even more important. That is the strategy, plans and tactics being activated by China. The Chinese Communist Party (CCP) is our opponent and following the Communist Marxist Manifesto "destroy Capitalism for the sake of a socialist benevolent politburo" that turns into a few controlling the many with fear and destruction of human rights and values.

"Man of the dart/spear," or alternatively "his death shall bring," *[1]* is the oldest person whose age is mentioned in the Hebrew Bible. Extra-biblical tradition maintains that he died on the eleventh of Cheshvan of the year 1656 (Anno Mundi, after Creation), at the age of 969, seven days before the beginning of the Great Flood.*[2]* According to Rashid on Genesis 7:4, God delayed the flood specifically because of the seven days of mourning in honor of the righteous Methuselah. Methuselah was the son of Enoch and the grandfather of Noah. The name *Methuselah*, or the phrase "old as Methuselah," is commonly used to refer to any living thing reaching great age.

Webster defines longevity as a long duration of an individual's life. It's the how many years of what you are, who you are, when you are in the short duration of history. Does it really matter if those celebrities are in the public's eye and complain that they want to be left alone? Not really, 100 years from now. Who was Caesar anyway? Was he a shortstop with the Cubs or White Sox?

Our world will be based on how many years are shown on our gravestone, not how many sexual encounters we had. Ego is a life-shortening, gut-wrenching, "sorry for ourselves" troublemaker in the long run of things. Is longer better than wider, or is fame bigger than what you have done for your family? Who cares if you are on the cover of *Rolling Stone* when it is no longer relevant to the future? Longevity or brevity is up to each, his/her own, isn't it?

The point being; for our own self-health there needs to be an appreciation of what we have accomplished, in keeping with our natural self-health that we inherit from the natural universe of time.

Then, it must be applied in a learning mode:

1. How to make friends.
2. How to be a good father or mother.
3. How to be a good teacher of others.
4. How to be a gift to society.
5. How to be a leader versus a complaining follower.
6. When to stand up and when to sit down.
7. When to begin and when to bow out.
8. When it is too late to fool with Superman's cape.
9. Where you fit in the bigger picture.
10. Where you fit in the smaller picture.

Making Friends

Grade school was the start of making friends for me. The kids in my neighborhood all went to the same school as I did and the bonding took place on the playground, and in the backyard. Any group has a leader and followers. Grade school was the first experience I had with leadership. Starting up a touch football game, a game of marbles, a game of hide-and-seek, a game of "tease the girls," a game of "who is on my team," a game of "anti-anti over the church steeple" with my friends.

Junior high school was more about girlfriends than it was about the boys They were teammates in sports, but not as enticing as the girls. The pairing up started in fourth grade with "she likes you" to "who is that" in eighth grade, to "will you go with me to the picture show" in ninth.

High school was the maturation of the body and spirit, called "falling in love with someone's look"; infatuation more than any commitment. But the juices were flowing and life became more about who dates who then true friendship. Sports stipulated who would make it competition rather than bonding for the boys. The girls, on the other hand, did make lasting friends. In the smaller communities, gangs and cliques had less of a hold on the individual than in the cities. Again, being a gang member or a Boy Scout did not represent a lasting friendship nor bring with it a meaningful family unit.

College was founded on individuality and did not pull either sex closer together except for dating and courting. The frats and sororities worked hard at bonding with their rituals and social events, but still little-lasting friendships that even came close to the bonding in grade school formed reasons for reunions but not permanent unions. Those are fleeting relationships at best. They are more for learning respect than what to expect after graduation to reality.

Therefore, the true lasting friendship is in marriage and commitment to family. Can you have friends otherwise? It would be stupid for me to say no. It is the very definition of friendship that I refer to. Webster says it is "one attached to another by respect or affection." Have you heard the phrase "absence makes the heart grow fonder"? The very essence of friendship is not absence, it is permanence. That is not just some acquaintance, it is someone you have bonded with, a wife and husband, a parent for life, building a heritage of love and friendship.

How to be a good father or mother

To my knowledge there is no class or checklist on "how to be a good parent." It is mostly on-the-job training, with mistakes abounding. Any accomplishments in this endeavor are based more on common sense or inheritance than intelligence. Life is a cycle out of control until control is learned.

Control, as established in my self-health book number one, "Never too Old to Live", is mental, not physical. The mind is the determinant of all we seek and find. So the mere birth of an offspring, in my experience, is truly eye-opening and demanding. That moment that someone else depends on you and your values, goals, friends, and loyalties will mold the next generation of you.

You have to want to be good for goodness' sake. Parenthood takes understanding, affection, and respect. The parent trap is trying to do it after divorces and broken promises. I have been fortunate to only have to manage my self-control in one set of family ties, not two or three. Those that do it in the nuclear bonding families have my sympathy and empathy at the same time. It is either complicated friendships or sinking ships, but just making it work is wonderful when it does. Longevity does not die with your death because each offspring has a piece of you for each generation for eternity.

How to be a good teacher of others

I have had my own small businesses for almost forty years and I keep learning the same lesson over and over: the only true friendship is built on teaching someone something of value and praising them for learning and then doing it. Ironically, the same is true for raising stable siblings.

I never considered myself a good teacher. I aspire to be but don't take time to map out a plan for teaching someone else friendship skills. I am not a backslapping, *rah-rah* sort of leader. I have high expectations and low accountability skills. Follow-through is the most important skill of a good teacher of others, and I had to learn to do that.

I overcome this by putting out fires. Not that I am proud of it; it forced me to change that bad habit. For your benefit, I would recommend having a checklist of what you are teaching to whom and follow up on their execution. It will nail down the friendship, ownership, and loyalty all at once. Teaching out performs preaching for an everlasting successful enterprise.

How to be a gift to society

The Bible and self-help books encourage "give to get." Do the giving before the getting and you shall forever be grateful. To me, this seems a little forward to think that giving is the only way to get. In my mind, it is more like intending to give than attending to the giving, not as the means to getting but the meaning of getting.

Confused? Well, our role in society is to be a steward of our talents and actions. Giving to society seems distant and impractical. What it is, in reality, is your intentions and attention to day-to-day details. Do you respect your peers? Do you respect your relationships? Do you abide by the rules? Do you question those that don't? Do you question the rules and find better answers to the questions? Are you a part of the problem or the solution? Is your glass half-empty or half-full at the end of each day?

Is being positive the hardest task on your checklist? It is on mine. The negative, cynical world affairs and happenings can bring you down to their level unless you focus positivity on your friends, your accomplishments, and hopes. That is your gift to society, being a problem solver, a positive force for better, a voice for reason, not reaction. This attitude will live on in your epitaph.

How to be a leader versus a complaining follower

Lead me, follow me, or get the hell out of the way. Leaders are made, not born. Leaders are benevolent, not mean. Leaders are fearless, not cowardly. Leaders are sincere, not unscrupulous. Good leaders are rare, they are not around every corner. Aspiring leaders are everywhere, on the school ground, in the park, on the stage, around the next town, over the next bridge, everywhere in America, around the world.

The problem is there are followers following followers who claim to be leaders, going nowhere fast. It does make a difference as to where the pack is going. Gangs prove this equation. They are led by leaders going nowhere but down into the gutter. Political leaders who are self-enriched for the sake of fame and fortune are, and many are taking us all into the gutter. Business leaders who ignore the rules of law are stealing from society. Bureaucrats who make their own rules for the sake of power and controls are destroying private-sector jobs and equity.

So, what are you aspiring to be? A leader for the right reasons and dedicated to those followers or one that takes advantage and has little respect for the team or the mission? We all saw the movie about "build it and they will come." "Field of Dreams," just do it with faith and everything turns out right, right? Wrong. It only turns out right if the right people do the right things at the right time. Timing is everything, I have been told time and again. So, leaders must determine the time for the right effort then lead others toward that outcome. And then be willing to make right those mistakes, start over and over until the team succeeds in accomplishing the mission. Proving that enterprise lives on with historic and ethical minded leaders.

When to stand up and when to sit down
(know when to hold and know when to fold)

The saying "know when to hold 'em and know when to fold 'em" is classic when it comes to enterprise. Businesses start and fold every day; 60,000 start each month and 60,000-fold each month that's 720,000 risk takers innovating and creating new products and services who will get the chance to start again. (America's bankruptcy law is unique in that it allows risk takers to try and try again ... America rule of law is the only country in the world to allow for failure to encourage taking a chance for success). Work and risk taking makes the world go round and taking risk rewards the risk takers with more than money. For example, Senator Bird lived into his nineties as long as he worked for his passion. The day he stepped down is the day he no longer stood for the reason to live and died shortly thereafter. He was in public service but still withstood attacks on his risky decisions and was rewarded with respect.

All of us will be faced with this type of decision; the when is in our hands, the why is in our minds, the result will be ours to live on with. We should not shorten it for rest or the promised "Life of Reilly" because it does not exist, unless that is all we want in our pursuit of longevity. A life lived long is a life lived on the edge of tomorrow, not on the dread of today or the unhappiness with the past. Make today lived your way, not because of pay or how we pray, but what you have wanted to do all your life. Take the risk and you will be rewarded with longevity.

When it is time to begin and when to bow out
(purpose is knowing how to begin and how to hold on)

We begin our life's journey with hope and ambition. As a child, everything seems possible and nothing scares us other than the threats created in our minds by our parents or peers. The more we hear, the more we fear, until nothing seems near and attainment seems too far until our ventures into school projects and sports open up an avenue for expressing our dreams. And unless they are stymied by the critics or realists who are cynical about making efforts that don't feed the ego, we have a purpose.

Purpose, goals, and reasons to work are established early with the ethics learned from our parents. However, if the values learned are short on truth, honesty, and effort we must learn it the hard way or not at all. It is no one's fault but ours if we just follow our habits, because that is just the way it is, because there are always choices. Do we stay in school, take that job, marry that person, have that next drink, take it before they take it from me, live on the edge of the law and outside the family or strive to make all things better and all days happy?

Beginning and staying on the right path is always a difficult choice if there are obstacles such as disability, injury, bad luck, poor health. Most of us have one or more of these during our life, some more than others. Just look around and feel fortunate to be happy, healthy, and prosperous. If you cannot, then you need to reassess your values and habits so the journey does not take you into that dead end. Bowing out of bad habits and attitudes for a better outcome requires that you begin again by determining mentally how you are responding and reacting to problems, obstacles, and taking small steps to better days. It's your journey and your time to be happy, healthy, and prosperous forever after. Amen.

When it is too late to fool with Superman's cape

Politics are not for the good fellows. Our system of government does not lend itself to discourse. Bigger is better. Small is broke. The middle is out of luck. Money talks and influence listens. However, America works its butt off for the American Dream of having money and influence. In many ways this is evolutionary, and minds change and times slowly form justice. But in the meantime, wasting energy on those things that one person cannot change will wear you down.

The difference between the politician and the business person is businesses take on problems rather than issues. Our Superman system is not looking for change in the same way that businesses change direction to solve problems. This is because there is no effective form of accountability or the drive for improving quality of life. Our senators, representatives, governors, councilmen, mayors find themselves in the spotlight, and no matter the decisions, it is not their money they are spending. It's not their fault that the people don't work hard enough or smart enough to pay taxes and keep quiet.

So, to be working for a purpose is what the books recommend, while reality says don't get involved. Most of us want to have a say but don't speak up. All of us complain but don't step up. Somewhere in the middle of all this is the secret to living with it and loving America in spite of its flaws. Our collective mental health depends on it. When we abdicate our personal responsibility to politicians, we are actively destroying the American Dream's longevity. So, vote for a purpose not a party.

Underlying all of this is the reason to "never quit" because if you do that a diamond will be found by some else, less capable.

Where do you fit in the bigger picture?

Down home in hometown America lies the heart of our country. We get the news from the media owned and operated by big business. Big government, big business, big pictures are dumbing down the rest of us. CNN, Network News, MSNBC, etc. commentators are all from out there, not down here. They are generally intellectuals and younger liberals wanting to interpret what is important to the masses. We see them as unreachable. Watching the Sunday pundits expound on what America thinks and does is an insult. There are conservative forces at work to counter the liberal leaning of the media such as Fox News, News Max, radio hosts Rush Limbaugh, podcasts such as mine the American Enterprise Manifesto. But we have a diverse public that are wedded to their party and beliefs waiting for something better.

Why? Because, they still are subjected to arrogant responses of "well, look now," "now listen," "if you hear me right," "if you think about it," "if you only knew" are insulting our perspective of what is fact or fiction or just opinion. Fitting into this chain may never change, but accepting that we the people should be governed by the elite, the intellectuals, the smart people, is not the formula for a healthy country or the pursuit of happiness, the root to longevity. And just accepting it as untouchable is not a democracy anymore. It is out-of-touch insanity. In my self-health approach, it will be established that those that find a way to have their voices heard live longer than those that are talked down to.

If you feel out of touch with your life and cynical towards the Big Brother government and the Brotherhood, all it takes is to join a movement supporting a third-party representing individuality and Humanism … the humanitarian American Enterprise Party.

Where do you fit in the smaller picture?

Fitting in is what we wanted in high school, not the rest of our life. Trying to be liked—respected, yes, but not loved is the problem. We all seem to want to be appreciated for what we do and yet it eludes most of us. However, America succeeds and fails on the small picture, not the big picture. Of the over 300 million people, if only 1 percent are happy, then the other 99 percent will make dramatic changes. Just look at Libya, Syria, and Egypt. What about China, North Korea, Russia, Iran, et. Will they live on as communists or realize democracy is a reason for revolution for longevity.

Encouragingly, recent polls cite that most Americans are happy with their current state and their future, so we are still in the game of living longer. However, if you believe in the inevitable rise and fall of societies, America's decline in education, standard of living, employment, retirement finances, housing, and jobs is endangering our nation's longevity. So, whether we are in small-town America or the city, just accepting the decline as a recession or temporary economic downturn is avoiding the problem. We are the small picture that makes up the big picture.

Salvatore Dali's greatest work, in my opinion, is his portrait of Abraham Lincoln made up of hundreds of small pictures of a nude woman. At a distance it was just the big picture of Lincoln, but the closer you got reality set in, with each small picture making up the bigger vision. My point is, being the small picture makes you an important part of the bigger picture if you put it in the right perspective. Your vote does count. Your voice can be heard. Your longevity depends on it because you create reality, reality does not create you. But collectively we sustain the big picture in our small ways … like the tide makes a sea the best government is one that honors each individual.

Hierarchy of the Work Ethic

Birthright, born in America, immigrant, illegal alien, taxpayer, citizen, employee, employer, boss, investor, banker, accountant, lawyer, etc. We, as Americans, have the right to work and to fail and to try again. Those that choose to find easier means of survival will not reap the benefits of American enterprise. So taking the right to work is the first step in the hierarchy of the life and work ethic needed to succeed in enterprise.

Values and Virtues, on the other hand, are the motivating factors for your work versus play. Do you want a high standard of living? Do you want an education? Do you want to be better than you are? Do you practice your trade? Are you trustworthy to yourself and others? Are you honest about your actions? Are you in love with yourself and others? All of these traits are learned and earned, while play only requires time and money, results of the virtuous work ethic. The choice is always yours.

Education is the seed planted in a fertile mind that grows an idea, a plan, an action, a business, a successful career, a happy family, and a meaningful work ethic. Dumb and Dumber found that the lack of intellect is humorous but not for going anywhere or accomplishing anything; it is just play at its best. Don't get me wrong, play is necessary for living a fruitful life but not an ethical life. Chances are, the higher the education, the higher the standard of living and the higher the arc of achievement. Those who sacrifice learning for play or pay shall eternally be poor.

Each action and reaction give us the right to work and then enters the reason and result of work. The reason, in my mind, is not about money, fame, or fortune but our self-satisfaction. Maslow's hierarchy of needs lays out the pyramid, with survival as the base, ego, satisfaction, actualizing as the hierarchical building blocks of life. To be able to even build a meaningful life takes preparation, meeting 10,000 hours minimum invested in becoming an expert, according to author Malcolm Gladwell, to attain the result of work's excellence. **Preparation meeting opportunity** is the definition of being in the right place at the right time, or more conventionally, *luck*. There is no pride in winning Lotto but winning the race to capitalize on the life and work ethic is fulfilling and satisfying. First for quality sake in the race for then set your own pace.

Can we have money, fame, and happiness? Ask those that have **money and fame** if they are happy. Most times they are not working for ethics but for pride, satisfaction, but not finding the hierarchy of making a difference in others' lives. It is protecting what they have and seeking security instead of actual self-worth. The scale and hierarchy of work is not that security is eluding us, it is that we lose sight of the value of our work to others. In a sense, receiving **benefits and security** without much effort distorts our values and gives us a distorted view of what we feel is owed us, not a result of the life and work ethic but of a false sense of security.

In effect, all of this is evolving every day for every American in different proportions, without us knowing why. Evolution for better is seeking the right fortune for the right **future unfolding** in a society that recognizes work as an asset, not a burden. Our forefathers worked for a different reason than most of us do today. Theirs was for survival of the fittest and to be able to live past thirty years of age. Now many attempt to scale Maslow's hierarchy, thinking we have the birthright to succeed without the right work ethic.

To **make a difference** in others' lives in a positive manner takes thought processes different from those of the baby boomers, millennials or the X, Y or the Z generations engendered. It appears, we as a society, have gone back to Roman values where thrills, reality shows, the have and the have-nots, the control by the governing bodies are destroying the work ethic, with the new entitlements of minimum wage, workers' comp, unemployment benefits, food stamps, welfare-guaranteed pensions, child care credits, unlimited healthcare. We no longer can afford research and development or pensions in our small businesses that do in fact create 90 percent of the jobs and teach the life and virtuous work ethic and risk-taking behavior to their offspring.

By living the 10 standards of behavior

Thou shall not kill
Thou shall not commit adultery
Thou shall not steal
Thou shall not bear false witness
Thou shall not covet your neighbor's wife
Thou shall not covet your neighbors' goods
Honor your mother and father
Worship the Lord our God
Thou shall not take the Lord's name in vain
Keep the Sabbath day holy

These 10 standards cross all line-s
Of race
Gender
Religion
Geography
and Politics

LIFE IS BUT A GAMBLE

Life is but a gamble fraught with danger
Gambling every day
What you're willing to wager
Is what life will pay

If you demand
That it pay you more
Or pay you less
You must move the pieces
In the mortal game of chess

So put your money down
Put your life on the line

Accept the reward as earned
And don't regret and whine

For if you choose
To beg and borrow
Hoping for much more
You're destined for the sorrow
Sibilant sounds of a whore

Put your money down
Put it on the line
If you wager for a crown
I hope you risk more than a dime

For if your gamble is too small
And it doesn't justify your wants
For pity you will fall
Into the heap of the has been debutants

To profit more than you sought
Make your effort with all you've got
Put it on the line with faith
You will receive what
You gambled knowing risk can wait

Beyond waiting for the beginning
Ending the feeling of elusive happiness
Gambling in life is for winning
Instead of fearful stress

Reminiscent of the line that said
"I gambled life for a penny
And life would pay no more
I gambled life with thoughts of winning"

With ethical profits and many rewards that await galore

LIFE TOO BIG TO FAIL

So, what happened to …

Small towns are better
Work forever for the same company
Be a patriot
Love thy neighbor
Pledge allegiance to the flag
Pray to God
Save 10%
Give 10%
Believe the media
Honor your parents

Life was too small to fail

Life then was what it was … just right

How do we get it back?

Pe Ten Commandments of Life

Focus on family
Bring talk back to the dinner table
Play together stay together
Love our spouse for better or worse
Pride in our work each day
Support our political leaders and police
Kneel to pray stand to pledge allegiance
Give thanks to our maker
Enjoining ourselves in matrimony
Sow and grow the roots of a family tree
Pen life is too big to fail

(The next nine chapters propose a way to recover the life and work ethic that makes American Enterprise great today and tomorrow.)

LIFE IN MY SUIT

A maker bred me with his hands
A tailor thread me with his hands
A baker fed me with his hands
A preacher wed me with his hands
A teacher led me with his hands

A woman said she loves me with her hands
All bled life into my suit
Now my hands treat that fruit
With excess abuse and misuse

Without regard to its origin its tailor
Its breadwinner its sanctity
Its sustenance its best friend
Which is its longevity considering mortality's brevity

Except with a maker of my coffin
My eulogy
My burial ground
My last will and testament

Yes it's a restatement of my life

A maker takes me with his hands
A tailor prays for me with his hands
A baker cooks my last supper with his hands
A preacher eulogizes me with his hands
A teacher remembers me with his hands

A woman says she loved me with her hands
All bled life into my suit
Now my hands treat that fruit
Without excuse and no misuse

It takes a free country to give me an excuse
For I now have heaven as my recruiter or hell as my suitor

Charter Two

Work for the Sake of Living—Building Character

Love What You Do, Do What you Love"

L ive	**W** ants
I ove	**O** ffer
F or	**R** esources
E ver	**K** indled

Love of Work and life's wants are bedfellows. Would we work if we did not want resources for our kindling to fire up our standard of living? Or does the want to work evolve out of our desire to live for something, i.e., self-respect, self-worth, self-esteem or just love of life?

I remember hearing associates dream of being successful so they could retire early at forty to fifty. Then it seemed lackadaisical and lazy thinking; now, with the current economic conditions, it is impossible to attain that status unless you are a street person or an extremely wealthy person.

Why work when there is play? Why play when there is comfort? Why comfort when there is no responsibility? Why irresponsibility when there is boredom? Work, in my opinion, is to avoid boredom and lack of purpose for self-respect. Adam Smith Wealth of Nations … "It is better, says the proverb, to play for nothing than work for nothing. In mercantile and manufacturing towns where the inferior ranks of people are chiefly maintained by the employment of capital, they are, in general, industrious, sober, and thriving".

What does the human being really need for a fulfilling life? Rank these top ten pieces of gold for your use in attaining a fulfilling life:

1. Money
2. Success in work
3. Notoriety
4. Celebrity
5. Role model
6. Self-Respect
7. Family
8. Love
9. Happiness
10. Health

A recent study showed that you can invert the list and have what most people really want. So, work ranks ninth in our true wants but most of us think it is the way to accumulate money, which creates happiness. However, that study also showed that as we age the inversion reverses itself. So, money is back on top and work moves up to second. Why would this be? Because the resources are being depleted and we feel that our health and happiness is beyond our control.

What if you are never too old to work and health is not last and happiness is not ninth? Isn't that the essence of character building and stability? Put yourself first. Right now, I am approaching 82 and didn't retire until 75 while saying I'm in rehire to have a purpose and goals.

I am not an expert on work and I am not an expert on aging, but I am doing both until I die and I expect to die like Methuselah with no regrets. Work does that for me. It is another form of healthy living and happiness if we are doing what we love. It is an honor to have all three.

Is work, as a love affair, possible if you have not or cannot choose how you spend your time? Ironically, you always have a choice if you choose to, so the love affair is within your reach no matter how far the target. It just depends on your insight, vision, and determination. Not easy, but feasible to every human being's brain and body.

What do you currently love to do? Make the list and see if you have them. If not, make a choice or what you are going to do to attain the love affair with what you really want. The book "The Secret" by Rhonda Byrne termed the Law of Attraction used to find what you love… in my case it was my attraction to my wife of 62 years when she was in seventh grade and I in eight. But it took four years to get a date with her. Two years we were married and have 32 offspring to prove the Law works.

Therefore, using the Law of Attraction, mine are the above top ten in reverse; money last, health and happiness first, which enables me to have a stable family, be a legend to them, be a role model to them, be a celebrity for my grandchildren, be famous for being the youngest looking person to reach 100 years, and the proof that work does matter to longevity. The money to live this way will come in the form of resources kindled by my want to be healthy and happy.

BORN TO EARN IT

All of us want self-respect

But self-respect
Isn't free
For all
It's earned

By earning self-respect
Some learn it
Some spurn it
Some burn it
Some earn it

But most don't realize
It's right before their eyes
If their attitude buys
Self-respect in disguise

It's not free
For all must grow it
It's earned
By growing self-respect

Selling disrespect short
And anti-abort
Isn't the resort
When the expectant
mother is in court

And the child has no escort
Or the father's the sort
To not take on support
Imposing a tort

Then the mother has to earn it
Even being born to an itinerate
Buys no self-respect
The child still has to earn it

No other way to get it ... just do it
For it builds character

CHARACTER

Character is what a blind man begs
In his darkest conceits
A cripple has in his legs
A dreamer in his defeats

Given that, no character is from living
But must be gained
Through pain and giving

Then only those that suffer
Can make a claim
On pain and Character

Building a character flaw
May result in the creation of
A prison not a Cathedral

Be careful that your painful decision
Doesn't draw you in
And imprison your indolent passion

That could gain conjecture
About your entrance to the hall of fame
Of a Cathedral to your Character

For overcoming blindness, darkness
Crippling disease and defeats
Is the true Statesman of greatness

As recognition always comes later
Then ambition

Charter Three

Goals versus Objectives—Building Initiative

"Just Do It" . . . Nike

The greatest self-help books of all time tell us to have goals to achieve our objectives that we conceive and believe; confusing when we are facing unemployment, foreclosure, and financial insecurity. Where do we start when there seems to be no hope?

H ealth

O ffers

P ersonal

E energy

Health on earth comes from working for what we want. The objective is to feel happy and the goals to do so are your activity. Believe and you will receive, give and you will achieve, conceive and you will have hope. The mind works on this principle for all human beings. According to the Bible, the greatest minds, the richest people, the legends are from our own aspirations.

The church of our existence is found in our subconscious mind, waiting to be trained in hopeful plans and feeling good about the goals we have achieved. The negative mind is not working on these levels, they are looking for outside circumstances to change so they can be positive and happy—doesn't seem to be working for inmates, criminals, porn stars, street people, addicts, and those that have given up.

How can we solve the problems that cause the loss of hope?

- Unemployment: look for a job that pays something and then make it your purpose to be the best at that job ever. You will be rewarded for being different from everyone else that is looking for the better job, and you will be the one who gets it.

- Foreclosure: tell the bank that you have a plan for paying your mortgage payments and then tell them what you are willing to take out of your bank account each week. This commits both of you to finding a way to solve the problem.
- Financial insecurity: there is no magic formula when there is not enough to go around. According to the financial experts, who are always current on their own bills, look at the smallest possible payment solution and propose it to your credit card companies, contingent on them lowering the interest rate and late charges. Then double the actual payment for six months, then request a further reduction in the periodic payments and interest rate.
- Remember that insecurity, lack of hope, and fear are lowering your capability to achieve your goals. Feeling good is your biggest asset in believing you can achieve the plan you have personally conceived. Take every negative thought and turn it around, because 85 percent of your worries never happen and the other 15 percent are only half as bad as you have conjured them up to be. The odds of 7.5 percent should not prevent you from becoming what you want to be.

The following are work exercises that will earn your way out of debt:

1. Plan to love your work no matter what; take the initiative to be the best at what you do and believe you can be. This can help in finding jobs as well as keeping jobs.
2. Plan to believe you will solve your financial problems with specific actions at work to reduce your dependence on credit.
3. Plan to achieve your goal of being happy and healthy and prosperous in your current job.
4. Plan to conceive ideas that will improve your work environment and job requirements.
5. Plan to succeed at being positive regardless of the obstacles and relish the fact you are an exceptional product of work. *Can't* never did anything and *can* invented the world.

6. Plan to age slower and more productively if you are positive about your efforts.
7. Plan for retirement using a savings or investment program to enable your family to live without dread of approaching the loss of employment because of age or early retirement.

My objective of honoring the life and work ethic changed over the years as I became the employer versus employee. I needed to be concerned about someone else's work ethic. How would I motivate another to do what I expected and when I needed it done? At first, I made it difficult because I was insecure in my own job so doubt was in the way. Then I realized both of us want the same thing . . . satisfaction, feeling of accomplishment and earning enough to pay the bills. And we both could accomplish our goals if we acknowledged them and helped each other reach them. It takes communication, cooperation and understanding to make it work . . . but that is what virtuous ethical work is.

My problem is, I avoided the thought of retirement and having my own business I thought that would be enough to cover my time to retire … it didn't happen that way. My wife, son and I owned three nursing homes and we didn't sell them until my wife and I were 75 and had to adjust to this slowdown in pace and passion. We have enough to fund retirement but we needed to take up my writing and Shari's painting to make life interesting and challenging. Also, our family had grown over our sixty years of marriage to 4 grown children, 12 grandchildren and 9 great grandchildren, so our focus was on that as well. It is our goal to be married another 15 to 20 years and capitalize on the opportunity that America provides us rehire possibilities if necessary.

IS BIGGER BETTER

Life is too big to fail

How big is God
He is the faith to do right

He's the patience to avoid wrong
He is the understanding to know the difference
Nothing shall be bigger than God

How close is happiness
Happiness is just beyond a positive step
Happiness is just around a smile
Happiness is just above a gleam in your eye
Nothing shall be closer than happiness

How deep is love
Love is life
Love is people and animals
Love is work
Nothing shall be deeper than love

How wide is truth
Truth is the goodness of youth
Truth is the righteous thoughts
Truth is sincere acts of kindness
Nothing shall be wider than truth

How far is death
Death is as close as life
Death is not a destination
Death is a life time journey
Nothing is any farther away than death

How long is life
Life is as you want it
Life grows as you grow
Life can be big deep wide far
Nothing shall be longer than life's final journey

How happy is marriage
Marriage is two finding one path
Marriage is one finding two turns

Marriage is three for mating two
Nothing sad about four more at the door

How big are children
Children are bigger than life
Bigger than husband and wife
Bigger than short or tall
Winter spring summer and fall

How big should government be
Too big if we aren't free
Too big if we hate our neighbor
Too big if the President hides the score
Too big if Congress is the ceiling and the floor

Pus Life is too big to fail
Unless our government gets too big
To care what's better
A tax or trend setter
A debt or interest payment
A deficit or Dow decent
A surplus or poverty
A war or prosperity
A solution or call it an issue

Because our offspring will perpetuate everything

Charter Four

What Matters Anyway—Building Security

Passion Creates Desire, Desire Creates Action, Action Creates Legends.

What really matters in life? Is it our past or our future? Is it our dreams or nightmares? Is it our lost loves or our current mate? Is it our job or our desire to be rich? Is it fear or our ability to turn risk into reward and hate into love?

P assion	**F** orming
A ction	**U** s
S atisfaction	**T** akes
T ime	**U** nbelievable
	R esources and
	E ffort

Our past is a passion of action, satisfaction, and times gone by. Our future is a passion of action, satisfaction, and times to come. Without passion, the past and the future create regret and hopelessness.

We all have a rap sheet. Sure, we all make mistakes and suffer the consequences. Is that pertinent to looking forward or is it to be forgotten and treated as a learning experience? The answer is up to you if you wish to make a choice. Most just accept the consequences as set in stone and do not knowingly take action to change the cause rather than the result. It matters most if we change the cause.

Our Past is Our Future:

"The mind can take you there" is the advice of the experts on the new mentality, which is really not new but old as Methuselah. Change in circumstances and overcoming current obstacles requires courage and faith, two characteristics that are many times inherited and not developed. However, the mind of a winner is the same mind of the sinner but the intention is different. The winner wants to better themselves while the sinner wants to make things easier and more gratifying.

Take your own intentions and make sure they are what you want to achieve, which does train your subconscious mind to pursue positive outcomes as its objective. The resulting goals are steps taken to be positive, with the faith to act on and stay on course with the plan.

> Example: mounting debt, dwindling resources, loss of job, and divorce—what in the world can be positive in that set of circumstances? Well, the conception of hope is that it takes the negative and puts it in a positive light (context) of feeling good about what you can control. This consists of your current income, your current job, your current relationships, your talents and abilities. It's all within your state of mind. State of mind is the only future you have, everything else is the past. The first step to sanity is to remove that which creates fear and apprehension by looking at the current controllable assets and the future plans. Starting with what you have is the most positive act you can make when all looks hopeless. In the book The Secret, by Rhonda Byrne, the Law of Attraction draws the solutions and outcomes to you in proportion to your belief in their occurrence. I too believe that what you can conceive is what you can achieve if you are so inclined and commit to that belief. In my experience to live any other way commits you to being the victim of happenstance and circumstance in your life time leaving unhappiness in its wake.

Our Day Dreams:

The most used word in the English language after *love* is *dreams. Aka the American Dream.* What you want for yourself is a mindful attempt to make the past better. The experts speak of envisioning the goal and attaining the objective, using dreams as fact and acting as if it has been achieved. Mental pictures of what is conceived are called *ideas* and *thoughts* when in fact they are visual dreams. While visualizing the future, activating can make the present pursuit of dreams into fulfilling goals. All of us use this power every day. We plan our day, we see the way with hope, and we remember our path through meditation to overcome fear of failure.

That is the pursuit of the American Dream with the willingness to fail and try and try again. America's bankruptcy laws promote the concept of surviving failure with starting over using a new approach with raising capital and making a profit. No other countries have such laws making us American entrepreneurs more likely to take a risk than we would be, if we couldn't start over. The bankruptcy law and its codes Chapter seven, eleven and thirteen allow a Trustee to approve a plan and guide the process until it succeeds or is deemed a final liquidation of assets to pay off a proportionate amount of debt.

KEY TAKEAWAYS:

The American dream is the belief that anyone, regardless of where they were born or what class they were born into, can attain their own version of success in a society in which upward mobility is possible for everyone. The American dream is believed to be achieved through sacrifice, risk-taking, and hard work, rather than by race, religion, creed, gender or circumstantial chance. Deemed humanism by the American Enterprise Party in its Manifesto.

Our Nightmares:

The American nightmare is fear activated in the sleeping minds create negative images in the waking minds. Webster defines it as a frightening or horrible experience, the opposite of day dreams. Our memory bank stores frightening or horrible experiences and plays them back when we are at our weakest state, usually sleeping. Usually, these recollections are not real, but they do scare us into not believing our daydreams.

What matters is the mind can play back the other side of what we want, probably the side effect of stress in our daily life. The fifth promise is "no worries" then take a pass to avoid risk.

However, deciding to take no or little risk puts you at the margin with everyone else who have opted out of the pursuit. Myself, I usually had nightmares about not going to class then having to take an exam, or getting lost trying to make a speech in public or fear of missing an important meeting. All of which I made a habit of always being prepared for any test, never missing class and over preparing for any presentation I made as a part of my speaking career. I had to overcome the fear of making a formal presentation to an audience or selling a potential client on my services.

KEY TAKEAWAYS:

The American nightmare is
Is a Big Brother President Joseph Robinette Biden transformation to a progressive America:

- Open borders letting emigration destroy American sovereignty
- HR1 open voting and S1 endorsement of harvesting of votes
- Higher taxes to fund welfare state
- Closed freedom of speech through Big Tec and Post Office surveillance
- Closed fossil fuel pipeline
- Closed fossil fuel exploration and land leases for fracking
- Green New Deal promising zero emissions by 2035
- White supremacy and climate change are America's biggest problems and priorities
- Anonymous complaints on policing and civil penalties
- Police to no longer have immunity
- Farmers of black, brown, American Indian, Asian, Pacific Islanders get loans balances forgiven (Injunction judged racist)

- Supporting CRT and 1619 Project subjects in public schools
- Supporting surveillance by Big Tech and USPS Post Office
- Capitalizing on a crisis called the Pandemic of Covid-19

America transformed in the first 100 days of the Biden administration into an oligarchy from a Trump monarchy run by the gang of 545 (100 Senators, 435 Congressmen, 9 Supreme Court Justices and 1 President).

Orwellian in its intent and substance as Washington burns while Biden, Harris, Pelosi and Schumer fiddles with Marxism.

Our Love/Soul Mate:

Human beings seek out mates for more than procreation. This expresses what really matters to the existence of humanity. Antilove, known as hate, expresses the worst of human existence. The evolution of mankind is based on the extension of love through family, faith, courage, and work. Divorce complicates the interaction of mates that seem to fall victim to hate and in reality, results in the lack of love. The more we understand that finding the soul mate is in the mind, not in the heart or the libido. In my case I saw her in Seventh and me in Eighth grade and didn't get her attention until my senior year in high school by chance on Halloween night 1956. We have now been married going on 62 years with four children, 12 grandchildren and nine great grandchildren thanks to the Law of Attraction. (Again, I suggest you read the book "The Secret" by Rhonda Byrne for finding your love/soul mate)

Our Job/Profession:

Schooling and education are directing us toward our dream job, until we realize that we have to suffer with our aspirations being stalled in a job that may not fit our dream. This is called experience and developing a skill. Talent is the factor that must be exercised so it does matter. It is said it takes 10,000 hours of suffering to develop talent to the extent that it matters more than desire. If we only knew when we graduate from the different levels of getting prepared, that we have to decide where we are going if we expect to get there. Each job prepares us for the next level of knowing when we are there. That's deemed our career and if qualified our profession which in my case was qualifying for a dream job out of college with Arthur Andersen & Co. in Chicago then eventually as a CPA with my own CPA firm and health care company, resulting in a forty-year career with hundreds of employees. Now it's my new career, writing about those experiences in health care, being an entrepreneur in American enterprise, innovating technology to solve problems in those fields affected by political leadership. The three volumes of The American Enterprise Party Manifesto represent a commitment to betterment of a wonderful philosophy of free market enterprise for all. The American Dream for those who honor work ethic and humanism.

Our Desire to be Rich . . . The American Dream is to reach acclaim with the riches of success and notoriety. Or is it the ego playing out what the soul never wanted in the first place? Are the celebrities the happiest people in America? Usually not. Who are the happiest people in America?

- New parents
- New grandparents
- Newlyweds
- New graduates
- Champions
- Lotto winners
- Business sharks
- Intellectuals

I would pick the top four and wonder how long it takes to find out that happiness can be fleeting and gone in a flash unless we have the first four. The last four are what we desire when we pursue wealth for the sake of being rich and forget what really matters. Happiness, good health, longevity, having hobbies to fall back on as we age and prosperity during or waning years. The Life of Riley or a fulfilling career as a professional may be the result of the American Dream job and marriage. In my case it resulted in all of the above.

Risk and Reward:

Life is all risk and reward, not just monetary but life itself. Every decision we make, consciously or not, entails risk and reward. If we contemplate this fact, we probably would not live for the right reason. We would live in fear of the unknown. Even though we would live less stressful lives, there would be very little purpose. What matters is our pursuit of health and happiness through our dreams and our work. The feeling of love brings down the reaction of hate and allows us to bring our dreams into reality.

That is the science of directing human behavior, that I call Humacology. that results in peace on earth, successful families, good health, happiness and prosperity. Take the chance that feels good in your heart. Take the equal chance that brings positive feelings to others. Civil rights are what really matters. Myself, I risked my future on the past experiences and enjoyed the rewards of successful businesses, a happy marriage with 32 successful offspring.

EQUALITY

The allegory that we are all born equal
Is puzzling since we are all different

Man is born to be equal
Not born equal
Not white not black
Not yellow not tan
Or red
It is only skin instead

Woman is born to be equal
Not born a man
Not born rough
Not tough
Not strong enough
Or gruff
It is only what is within her skin

So race or women take heed
Hear your calling
But remember your breed
We cannot have mares
Without the steed
And night mares
Without God's speed
In color and creed

Equality is only in the mind
Of the beholder
And by design
We all are getting older
And when it is time
To hear the bell chime
Being equal isn't worth a dime
It is the justice not the crime
It is the opportunity that is free

That makes the man and woman
and race equally
Sublime

(Equity on the other hand is our self-worth value to humanity)

CIVIL RIGHTS

Civil rights are the foundation
Of our democracy
And our standards
For human value

Uncivil rights are the foundation
Of demagoguery
And the violations
Of human value

Be it a racial problem
Religious problem
Geographical problem
Or a political problem

Then why do we continue
To reduce these to an issue
My point is these deviates
Our approach from our personal interests

Not focusing on the interests
Of those who are the subjects
While turned to objects
By reducing civil rights

To uncivil rights
This is the "gimme" factor
In the equation of equality
And inequality

Equality it seems to me
Is what you can gain not what you're given
Regardless of circumstances
Or obstacles in the way

And inequality it seems to me
Is what you can lose not what you deserve
Because of the "gimme" circumstances
And wanting it just your way

Just another cry out for peace and tranquility
That's civil rights with opportunity
As we are born free with equal
Rights to die equally dead with no sequel

Or instant Replay

Charter Five

Who Will Remember You—
Building Lifestyle for Work Ethic

"Memories are made of this, a kiss, a miss, a reminisce"

M ost
E thical
M omments
O ffer
R espect
I nfluence and
E even
S atisfaction

All is fair in love and war. All is made of blood skin and hair. We are human and need to be remembered. Memories, good or bad, make us better; mistakes made, corrections learned, for better or for worse marriages. Are the celebrities all we remember? Are the politicians just for show or never to know? Good philosophy but never practiced. We remember the good times and forget the bad unless it is forced upon us.

The mind is the database, the subconscious is the random-access instrument. The conscious mind is the retrieval software under the stress of circumstances and habits. How can we control our reactions when we have no time to think, reason, or weigh the consequences? Well, we have a memory bank based on our parents, their values, their beliefs, their experience and hopes. Heritage of and homage to our parents do not necessarily come naturally. Most times they surface later on.

Much of our upbringing hinged on don'ts, don't this, don't that. So, the do's were between the don'ts, do be careful, do your best, do come home safely, do have a good day. As we go off to school then to work, our responses are likely to be from the memory bank, not the prudent bank, not the financial bank.

I now remember that my most satisfying memories were not about money or being prudent. They are from sports, grades in school, promotions at work, and a successful marriage leading to a stable family life. Was this my plan? No. Was this according to my personality? No. Was this about being right? No. It was my upbringing more than anything. Although there was little expression of love or affection, there were no drunken episodes, no wild and frightening threats to my safety, no defeated feelings about the future. Mainly a solid work ethic with the willingness to take on responsibility of a family and my own business.

My father worked all his life for nominal wages and little responsibility. He once told me he wanted no responsibility at work, just put in your time and come home early was his life. My mother was just the opposite. She always wanted more and made life miserable for my dad. Neither had more than an eighth-grade education and did not have the ambition to better that. Somehow, I had just the opposite desires. I wanted to be a risk taker, a dreamer with bigger and better goals, taking on more than my abilities could take me. My mother said I always wanted to fly before I had wings. Which is a good start to broken dreams but hard work also can fuel persistence and eventual success.

So, work of any kind for me is sacred. It is an expression of my memories of feeling too short (my nickname was *Tiny* in high school) but wanting big accomplishments. In football I was third-string quarterback, always taking on the bigger guys and would never give in to them. In basketball, my coach said as the point guard I dribbled too much though I was the best shot on the team, so I was the frustrated sixth man. In baseball, as a shortstop, where size did not relegate me to the bench, I excelled with my speed and desire to be the best. I was the leading hitter, leading base stealer, leading RBI guy, and our team was conference champion.

After high school, organized sports were not feasible since I did not have all-star ability, so I participated in a tennis league as an A- player who would never give up and won more than I lost. I played in basketball leagues for a few years, more as a dribbler and assist guy than a star. I played in a 16" softball league as the right fielder (the weakest are in right field) and caught everything hit at me (no gloves allowed). The team was sponsored by the CPA firm I worked for and we were undefeated due to our 6'3" shortstop who could turn every play and hit the big ball a mile. But he couldn't beat me in tennis.

At work, I was not the star, maybe reliable but not the smartest (in my opinion, though I scored 100 once on a Mensa entrance test and scored 148 on a Tribune IQ test). Accounting was the game and bored was my name, so I mustered out and started my own CPA firm. Figure that out. But the work product was not the result of just numbers. I liked the use of numbers to make business decisions and create information systems that improved the efficiency of the workers and the profitability of the clients.

A lifestyle of family first, job second, enterprise a commitment to both became an obsession after losing my job for insubordination. The true feeling of loss is unemployment so our lifestyle changed when that happened. The family stayed in Morton, Illinois in our soon to be sold home while I moved to Chicago to resurrect our healthcare consulting business. It was there that my work ethic was tested because I had to rebuild as quickly as possible so the family could also relocate. I also had to overcome my loss of self-esteem while rebuilding the business with hope.

All of this changed when my business focused on the specialty of healthcare. Healthcare clients needed automation and improved documentation. I had an idea that we could create software that would guide the process rather than just report what had happened. So, for the next twenty-five years my various businesses invested millions in developing systems, software, and methods to be able to control quality and costs, not just react to them. Enterprise entered into my world in the form of raising capital and making room for innovation for the sake of the elderly. My mother-in-law was in need and my parents both had expired in a despicable nursing home.

We were traveling all over the country, converting nursing home to restorative care using the Medicare reimbursement program, utilizing software systems that Kip, my son, had programmed using my understanding of the regulations and court cases that required that the government pay for restoration rather than their narrow guidelines for younger and less complicated cases. We were helped by lawsuits that found the federal government guilty of depriving the elderly and disabled of their Medicare benefits (*Fox vs. Bowen*, 1986, and recently *Jimmo vs. Sebelius*).

A legacy of attempting to make a difference in an industry misdirected, in my opinion, and teetering on imploding took us to ownership. We owned three skilled nursing facilities that took its toll on why our peers are not what they need to be. The force of big government was thrust upon us full force as "big government rides again" (Volume II for the Impact of Government enforcement on small businesses). The challenge is the regulators do not look at the human side of the business, only the narrow interpretations of the rules designed to keep the costs down, accusing the private sector of fraud and abuse while they misinterpret the rules and regulations. See my books, *Restore Elder Pride, iUniverse*, 2012, *Failing Government Taketh Away, America in the Red Zone*, for more details.

STANDING WITH SELF-ESTEEM

Peace and equality is a state not a condition

We all stand in awe
Of being special
Being different

Many strive to stand out
And end up the same
As the crowd influence is spent

Yes they're all the same
Trying to be different
Ending up misspent

Punk cool stoned
Chasing the same dream
I'm doing it my way

With SELF-esteem
Built on a loving dream
That we all can have peace
As long as hope doesn't cease

Warlords and dictators
Resist the force of freedom
But the people are the instigators
If they don't standup for self-esteem
If those who are imprisoned
Rise up on their back legs
And overthrow what they've dissented
Waiting for destiny that fear begs

No amount of our country's
Desire to rehabilitate

History's fate
Futile esteem will dictate

As peace waits for all people Who
are standing with self-esteem
Peacefully this will redeem
The haters and warriors of futile esteem
With a lifestyle built on a dream (hope)

HOPE

Hope springs will

My definition of hope
Is a way of painting
A vision to cope
With life without a picture

Where there's hope
There's a will
Where there's a will
There's a way

Don't think me a dope
When I hug and kiss you
And call you hope

Because will's looking for security
To replace doubt
Which has inhibited me

And you're the best thing
I've seen to take it away
From what life can't bring

That's what I mean when I say
Don't turn your eyes or
Drop your arms before dawn

Cause it's by the will to
have you that
I've got the hope to go on
So don't think me a dope
When I hug and kiss you
And call you hope

For where there's hope in a day
There's a will
And our will,
Will find a way

Charter Six

Who Will Remember America—Building History

Stand Up for Something or You will Fall for anything: Save America!

C ommitment
O ffers
U ltimate
R eturn
A nd
G ains on
E verything

Who do you vote for? Who do you respect most? Who do you like? Who do you follow? Who do you doubt? Who do you dislike? All this comes from your memory bank of experiences. I, for one, at times have decided to not vote because I do not respect their aversion to yes/no answers and they just talk of issues between the parties, not solutions to problems we all have. So, I don't like compromise at the expense of the majority, and I would follow someone of principle without a doubt. What is there to dislike?

America has become, in my opinion, a country of people who feel they cannot make a difference and give in to the system, whatever that is. Our leadership is bent on conformity to their incestuous ways rather than defining our collective problems and then working on solving them. Technically, our form of democracy tanked twice when the Federal Reserve gambled with taxpayer assets by using high interest rates to quell what they deemed to be rampant inflation (exchange rates hiked by the Fed in 1979 and 2005-07).

As I stressed earlier, I liken the current situation in American politics and business to the one depicted by Orwell in *Animal Farm* where the dictator is run off the farm by the abused animals so the smarter boars and pigs could garner support to became a socialist state. Then comrades for equality under communism could not meet its output quotas. Then when the farm no longer could afford to pay equal wages, it became a fascist state to control the underpaid and unpaid workers. Then due to the need to trade with their neighbors the elite intellectual management teamed up with the other dictator farmers (for the good of the owners, not the greater good of the worker animals). When the seventh standard of equality was all animals are equal but some are more equal than others the farm animals were put back into servitude at the farm. Sounds strangely familiar with our Bigger is Better government, doesn't it?

When our Congress uses the monetary resources by taking taxpayer money and gambling away our capital system, then blames our enterprise system for the problems that the Federal Reserve caused by playing Russian roulette with the member fed funds rates for member banks, we then dissipate America's consumption-based economy to spiral downward. To correct this mistake, we need to fertilize the economy with funds that flow readily downward to stop the spiral. Rather than reforms that suck upward more tax dollars or print more dollars for stimulating public service projects and corporate giants that do not increase our gross national product, we must downsize government and privatize our institutions. As government forces resources upward, business enterprise shrinks; as resources are disbursed downward, business thrives. Otherwise, an authoritarian government will blame the people for nonperformance, then punish them for non-conformance, then annihilate them for insubordination.

Therefore, we need to reform government using the principles of Enterprise to lift the lifestyle and work ethic above our desire or attempt to control our destiny. This great American society can only prevail if we seed monetary resources downward to the individual brains, hearts, and souls. The great American piety can only be controlled if we economize the monetary seeds but do not squander or smother them.

- Government is necessary to percolate our economy, not overregulate it. Government is only necessary to protect the individual's rights to be free to think, work, and succeed as the seed for evolutionary growth.

- Government is necessary to define good, not enforce it; recognize the good, not divorce it; organize our defense, not build fences against it. Government must be founded on the participation of the private sector, not the wasteful and inappropriate nesting of public officials.

- The following is a repeat of many of the proposals put forth in Volumes I and II, so you can skim them or reread and remember them as the foundation of improving America's work ethic. This is the "How" we can reform our existing government and salvage the Enterprise for the sake of worker ethics and human welfare?

1. Government must be returned to "of the people, by the people, for the people" (town hall government is not what we need or want).

2. Downsize the government and privatize our institutions so we save our economy; money is not the reason we work but the result of our freedom and opportunity to succeed on our own will.

3. Give peace a chance; the militarization of our foreign policy must be directed as peacemakers not peace fore sakers.

4. Redirect foreign aid to domestic aid to seed our small businesses, the job makers. Stop regime change in foreign countries and support those who are moving towards democracy.

5. Replace the moniker of *lawmakers* with *job makers* by reducing encumberment and confinement of the flow of capital for enterprise designed regulations.

6. Tax individual and corporate net worth, not Forty-six different facets of the enterprising workers to seed the wasteful, dominant, ineffective, and uncaring Big Brother government.

7. Make the Federal Reserve Bank a federal agency that doesn't gamble taxpayer money to control the economy and destroy supply and demand using interest rates; save the honor and value of the dollar as the worldwide reference currency by downsizing

government and upsizing enterprise using recapitalization of the economy through assessment of individual and corporate net worth for pay down of lone and short-term obligations.

8. Privatize the promotion of a healthy America; it is the individual who determines health and welfare, not government. We must stop overmedicating and underdiagnosing health problems and pay for outcomes, not just incomes.

9. Reorganize the electoral process so the majority rules and encourage the expression of the third-party voice as the swing vote (middle stripe of reason in our flag) between the red and blue parties' conspiracy of controlling the American people. It only takes 5 to 10 seats in the Senate and 10 to 20 seats in the House to be the swing vote to garner equal control by the American Enterprise Party.

10. Elect government officials at all levels based on problem-solving initiatives, not speeches on issues between the red and blue parties' domination of our disappearing individualized spirit.

11. Direct the fifty governors that we want them to take up enterprise over regulations as their banner eliminating all obstacles to our future GNP. Basing it on enterprise, not taxation, gambling tax, sale and lease back of American property to foreign interests, managed competition, and indiscriminate public costs for pensions, perks and special deals for state officials.

In summary, we must act now before we become an impure version of other great societies who failed to reverse the dominance of the many by a few. The opportunity is the vitality of the enterprising America for the youth, the elderly, the disabled, the dreamers, the entrepreneurs, and the seekers of peace. Therefore, the voter must take a personal interest in and an active part in our governance. The proposed platform of the American Enterprise Party is based on the constitutional rights to pursue individual opportunities for work, education, housing, procreation, lifestyle, and the pursuit of happiness. To do this, 50 percent of Congress and legislature in the country need to be seated by the private sector.

We must move away from any ideology that dissipates our American Enterprise. We must honor it for the sake of individual rights to decide, ability to perform, desire to procreate, receive equal opportunity for housing, education, and jobs. We must again fertilize our economy with the American Enterprise principles constituted by Washington, Lincoln, Jefferson, Hancock, Franklin, Adams, Henry, etc. As they envisioned there would be new blood infused by the voters so all aspects of the nation would be duly represented. Those rights no longer exist, nor will they until we interject an effective third party with the swing vote to propose opposing alternatives.

WHO ARE YOU

Who are you bright or dark
What do you know
Make your mark
Before you go

Who are you
What do you say
Will your words be remembered
Someday

Will your purpose make history
Or misery
Will someone salute your name
Or will they spit on your memory
Pen left as you came

And bury your memory
With you heading for the infirmary
And then forget to wave
Or even visit your grave

(continued)

Now is for the endeavor
If but you react
And now is gone forever
Unless you express
Who you are
And what you know
As fact

Stand up in spite of flack
As your words portray the Act

IDEOLOGY

An idea involves one person
An ideology involves billions of faith

You can kill an idea
But you can never kill an ideology
An idea is a fleeting thought of the future
While an ideology is the culture from the past

We in America have democracy as an ideology
Pat is why we say we are the land of the free
Pough we have the criminal element that aren't
And others that are freer than others

Which ideology is right or wrong
Pat is the worldwide question
Pat is threatening us all
To be destroyed by an idea

Evolving from the past idea
Pat we on earth are here because of creation
Or some atomic infusion and conclusion
Deciding our fate and life's state

Ironically, we come from the same place
And will return to the same destination
Pough we cannot agree to how or why
It is certain we all will die

Pat idea for some will distort
Into a Koran or a Bible that builds faith
On being right or wrong
Not why we are one and the same

Leaving no one to resurrect or blame
Except those that are here for an idea
Not some courted ideology
For justifying the dropping of A-bomb

Pen the ideologists can swallow their last prayer

To the God and Satan that were never there

Charter Seven

What will be Enterprise Legacy—Building Pride and Patriotism

What will be Anarchy Legacy—Building Bigger Government

"Apathy is worse than sympathy, empathy, allergy or a short eulogy"
. . . Jerry Rhoads

L everaging
E nterprise human capital
G oes
A long with
C ivil enforcement
Y ou must comply with the Rule of law

The new entitlements of bigger government are

1. Unemployment compensation exceeding pay levels
2. Workers' compensation for mental health and physical health
3. Minimum wage raises from $7.50 to $15 or a guaranteed income
4. Disability
5. Government-paid healthcare
6. Family leave
7. Paid time off for jury duty
8. Food stamps
9. Welfare (child care credits and guaranteed income
10. Universal healthcare benefits – Obama Care
11. Free college

12. Reparation
13. Forgiveness of college debt
14. Stimulus checks

All designed to "Build Back Bigger Not Better" that drives up labor costs that do not produce a dollar more in sales and GDP. All are included in the cost of goods and services that we attempt to sell in the worldwide market, competing with China, Mexico, Argentina, Taiwan, India, Pakistan, Russia, South Korea, and other emerging economies that do not have these entitlements.

Many of the American companies have transferred manufacturing and technology services to countries that do not have these entitlements. No matter how much the unions claim that we have shipped jobs overseas because of NAFTA or CAGTA or whatever trade agreement we have struck, it is the high cost of these other entitlements that force businesses to seek lower overhead and cheaper labor off shore.

While we build up our weaponry, instead of our patriotic legacy, with no value added to our GNP at the rate of $800 billion per year taken out of the enterprise, more and more is invested in weapons of mass destruction that we never use. We fall further in debt and farther into the competitive hole. Then preparing for a military war when it is going to be a cold war of a trade competitive business as usual. The legacy is more than deficits, it is lower quality standards, it is slipshod processes, it is rationalized government regulations that threaten businesses rather than collaborate for the betterment of our position in the worldwide marketplace.

Peaceful coexistence isn't our legacy; it's our patriotic history and not our current diplomacy. Tactically we continue to force our ineffective use of taxpayer resources on other countries under the guise of foreign aid and military support. Be it in the Middle East or in Asia, our image has shrunk to that of Germany and Russia in the past. The Soviets, the Third Reich were war machines bent on scaring away competition in their quest for control of natural resources and wealth.

As a result, the American life and work ethic is also being relegated to that of dollars and cents, not quality of life or loyalty to the company. It is based on compensation, work time off, health benefits, and retirement benefits. Less and less is being invested in small-business ideas and useful technology that makes the middle-class less stressed. Unemployment at the whims of big government initiatives is driving the cost of living out of sight. Workers just want a job to lose so they can claim one years' worth of unemployment benefits then cycle back into the workforce with an attitude that businesses owe them that privilege. "Just give me the right to get injured and I'll file for worker's comp and then sue for more than the cost to heal."

I, personally, come from blue-collar and farming heritage and have never filed for unemployment, worker's comp, minimum wage, nor other excuses for not working hard. Do I have sympathy for the working poor? No. Do I have sympathy for the working mothers? No. Do I have sympathy for the recovering addict? No. Do I have sympathy for the dried-out alcoholic? No. Do I have sympathy for the illegal aliens that work for their families? No. Do I have sympathy for same-sex marriages? No. But I do have respect for them if they are willing to get back up and work for the good of themselves, because of the following principles that what make America great.

- The land of the free that allows us all to take advantage of opportunity and forgiveness of failure by honoring the virtuous work ethic.
- An economic system that forgives debt if the debtor will continue to exert the life and work ethic for the good of the enterprise system.
- A flag that represents our collective patriotism for the world of peaceful coexistence based on color blind humanism.
- A heritage of speaking English, paying our taxes, praying to a God, standing for the national anthem, respecting our President, Congress and the rule of law.
- Saluting our flag, respecting our military, believing in our media, holding the media accountable, holding our President, Congress and Governors accountable for budgets, deficits, debt

and reporting the condition of the country once a year as the State of the Union.

- Establish security domestically and abroad with border security and immigration control according to the existing laws and constraints.

SPEAKING OF CAMELOT

Deck the halls with boughs of holly
Fa La La La La La La
Speak the vows of folly
Fa La La La La La La

We often speak of Camelot
In voices of grandeur
But more often than not
Our pursuit is unsure

We often speak of Shangri LA
With words of love
Until the ice begins to thaw
Like righteous words from above

But too often we speak of fear
In voices trembling weak
Not so are we insincere
As much as not meaning what we speak

My dreams are mine to think
Kept in perspective light
And at no time can I sink
If my hope is bright

We often speak of Camelot
Pen forget that actions are facts

And more often than not
Dreams are dust in our tracks

So sing on Jester of life
A breadwinner naught
For folly is a begetters wife
And shallow words are fraught

With thought and prayers of Camelot
Be it a President who has taught
Us that it is likely or not
Pat happiness can be bought

Or a forgiving God
Taking away our able thought
Making reality seem like a fraud
For accepting Camelot

Deck the halls with boughs of folly
Fa La L
a La La La La
Speak the vows of Pollyanna
Fa La La La La La La

When all we wanted is what we sought
A family a job a home to be bought
Not a dream of whether we like it or not
For someone else's Camelot

PROUD

Our standing in life with the judge
Is marked by what we give
Many will come and those gates won't budge
To those empty hearted with no reason to live

Blessed be those mortals that glow
Glow like stars in the night
Having left in their paths to sow
The particles of themselves so slight

As parents and the fore bearers
You cleared the way for your heirs
They will remember you as theirs
And as the heritage of all their cares

Proud, you should be very proud
Of what you have given to history
That mortal being shouting from the crowd
It's your offspring meant to be

To be or not to be that is the reward
Endowed upon the good for deeds
Not those living by the sword
Directed towards immoral creeds

Thanks for the memory
Of visions to be great
Without fear of frailty
And creating a faithful legend not too late

Take the credit you deserve
And pat your pride be satisfied
For you've earned the righteous nerve
To say I've been I've had I've tried

Proud that my Children are my rib my side

EMANCIPATION PROCLAIMATION

President Lincoln proclaimed
Equality is in the hearts of each person

A sharing person
Is a caring person

A joking person
Is a poking person

A knowing person
Is a growing person

A crying person
Is a denying person

A praying person
Is a staying person

A negative person
Is a dark person

A positive person
Is a colorful person

A trying person
Is a defying person

Sticks and stones
May hurt my bones

Set me free by emancipating me
So truth proclaimed can never hurt thee

A patriot keeping America free

LIFE IN REVERSE

Have you ever wished that living should be rehearsed?

What you're thinking
Right now
Makes a difference

Only we humans
Have this volition
To improve our position

Only to realize
That we have wasted
Most of our lives

Why couldn't life
Have been in reverse
Rather a future to rehearse

With the hearse being first
And flying at half-mast
Before I'm in the past

With a vision of what
When and why
Each day we have to try

But then it would
Have been a bore
Knowing the final score

Rather than
Hiding our winning hand
With the wonder of our last stand

With risk out of the fray
Why would we want to pray
About not getting old and gray

Most of us don't want the fuss
With life running us
Come hell or bust

But my reason here
Is to get you to steer
Your life and your career

By knowing you're the difference
You're the thinker
And the change maker

For when you're the trend setter
The world will be greater
Because you're better

But why couldn't life
Be rehearsed
Putting the future first

Because disappointment can't be last

Charter Eight

When Are We Most Happy—
Building Faith, Confidence and Civility?

Is Happiness Winning Lotto, Being Number One, Super Bowel champ,
Having a Hit Record or Show? Or being civil, patriotic and productive?

H onesty	**C** are
A pplication	**I**nstead
P rimes	**V**iewed
P ride and	**I**n
Y ields self-worth	**L**ove

I got my first job in Indianola, Iowa delivering newspapers around the town square then to homes on the weekends. After that the jobs were sacking groceries and pumping gas. So, jobs are not only necessary for making a living, they also put you into the American Enterprise system. This is the American Dream, make a living, growing a future, and feeding the family. Work is for the mind as well as the bank account. Getting an education is to further develop a skill for a job. The majority (90 percent of Americans work regularly to produce products and services that drives the enterprise wheel) support the world's economic machine. Our consumerism has made the world wealthy and will continue to do so as long as the American worker is healthy, wealthy and happy.

Happiness in the job is not the same as the happiness at play. For me it was the way to advance and pay for material comforts. The job was important to the whole pursuit of love, security, faith, feeling whole. Now that is being threatened by the recessions, depressions, strikes, and the economic rollercoaster. Our leadership have their job security due to wealth, status, social ignorance, and the majority's preoccupation with their own problems, most of which are imposed by the leaders. Will our satisfaction with the opportunities in America be destroyed by the system we have ourselves inherited?

Ethical work and civil workers:

Does a positive, civil life and work ethic necessarily produce ethical work? Which comes first, the chicken or the egg? The time or the clock? The air or the wind? God or Heaven? Here on earth or later? These are great unanswerable questions but,

- Does it really matter or is it better to work ethically as the reason and civil outcomes as the result? The means justify the end product. Then we have heaven on earth.
- If we lived and worked ethically with civility, as individuals, the work product would evolve ethically, but the ethical output has to be produced by workers who believe in quality and ethics.

From Adam Smith's *Wealth of Nations* to the Bible, ethics, principles, honesty, civility and caring all contribute to economies. Men and women are the vehicle with faith and ambition as the fuel with the engine being the pursuit of happiness, which is the ultimate wealth.

The family unit based on an ethical marriage produces ethical and civil offspring who sustain that reason for work. For work is not an option, it is the reason for living with health, happiness, and prosperity as the result.

Why then do some sustain that effort and others do not? In a free environment, each individual has the responsibility to sustain ethics in a civil manner or suffer dire circumstances. The results are always justified by the reason. Not justifying the result by any means is unethical.

America enterprise is the best example of the need to sustain ethical and work for civil reasons. The so-called American Dream is founded on ethical work for ethical reasons. The attained dream is the personification of ethical work with civility.

How, can we define ethical work and a civil ethical worker?

Ethical life and civil work:
1. Is the work product contributing to positives life outcomes?
2. The tactics are consistent with positive human values?
3. Tangible or intangible, does the work product sustain happiness, health, and prosperity?
4. Is the end work product contributing to the gross national product and national pride?
5. Would we miss the work product if it were no more?
6. Is the family interested in their parents work and understand work ethics

Ethical civil workers:
1. The individual who believes in quality-of-life principles (healthy, happy, and prosperous).
2. The human instinct to preserve our being is the priority, not a bad dream.
3. Positive effort is respected and reward is coveted.
4. Faith in pursuing positive goals and feeling good about attainment.
5. Able to change directions for the sake of others.
6. Thinks beyond today's problems by working for civil solutions.
7. Knows that each worker must desire their fate and live with the consequences.
8. The family is the most important reason to be an ethical and civil worker.

We all must seek and work for our future and not dwell on the past or we will relive its consequences.

When I joined Arthur Andersen & Co., CPA's right out of college I lacked confidence due to a lack of experience in accounting. Of course, they presumed that for all new accountants and put us through a four-week boot camp where many of the job candidates left before we were pledged into the firm. I survived by leaning on others for help and encouragement. It was like my first year in football . . . the freshman had to help each other just to survive the bigger and better players in scrimmages. This built confidence in my ability to survive any situation which carried me through the accounting boot camp. Since then, I have never feared trying something new and challenging such as starting my own business. My daughter warned me that I should take care of my health because I could not afford to miss work since I was the only worker . . . at that point my life and work ethic, of never missing work in 37 years, set in and has not waivered since.

The pursuit of faith and confidence eluded me for my first five years in auditing because, as I found out later, the job was inhibiting and not very challenging to the creative juices. It was not until I realized that my knowledge in Medicare and Medicaid could carry me far, that it dawned on me to exercise my entrepreneurial talents. The law of Attraction where likes attract likes and dreams sought can be dreams caught became my drive towards an ethical and civil business career in my own business. Though I was never drafted or served in the military due to having a family to support, I believe in being a patriot by supporting peaceful coexistence with no feeling of being a WASP supremist or superior to any person.

DEATH OF FEAR

Confidence comes from the death of fear
And it's not certain
When your self-esteem is hurting

Death of fear is certain
If you confront the fear you're averting

Death of self is sure
If you feel impure

Death of attitude is guaranteed
If your self-image you impede

Death of life is not inbred
Unless you believe you will be dead

Death is dread and doubt
That's what confidence is all about

So take yourself by the hand
Lead yourself to the promise land

Tell yourself that you understand
Give yourself an enthusiastic hand

With a prayer at your command
Doing what you know you can

For confidence is certain
When you can do what you're averting

CIVILITY

Webster defines civility as civilized conduct
(Especially: courtesy or politeness) or a polite act or expression.

Be it diplomacy
Or politically correct
Or being civil
Or being uncivil

Civility is not just being politically correct
Not going along to get alone
Not promises without accountability
Not spending money without availability

Then why do we continue
To reduce everything to an issue
If it's a festering problem in the way
And our leaders dilute it to a foray

Just go along to get along
Inequality results in uncivil laws
Uncivil rights
When we humans let relationships
Be decided by Government
Equality only starts with civil rights
Without uncivil laws
Intruding on the relationships
Required to love thy neighbor

By living the 10 standards of behavior

Thou shall not kill
Thou shall not commit adultery
Thou shall not steal
Thou shall not bear false witness
Thou shall not covet your neighbor's wife

Thou shall not covet your neighbors' goods
Honor your mother and father
Worship the Lord our God
Thou shall not take the Lord's name in vain
Keep the Sabbath day holy

These 10 standards cross all lines
Of race
Sex
Religion
Geography
and Politics

Civility isn't free but a necessary decree
From sea to shining sea
For every citizen to be free
To pursue equal opportunity

Ethically and civil for you and me

Charter Nine

How Many Years of Prosperity Are Left—
Building Staying Power

The whole world wants to retire in America,
but retirement cannot support the whole world

R ealize
E very
T ime
I nnovation
R epeats
E verything gets better

Retirement has been placed by us mentally at sixty-five years of age if you are ordinary and sooner if you are financially successful. Our Social Security system is based on the concept of sixty-five being too old to work and we should move out of the way for the younger generation. Is it working now with seventy-seven million Americans (the boomers) reaching the magical day of fulfillment at the rate of 10,000 per day and are wanting to take it easy? Politically and economically, this endgame is backfiring as our entitlements have made promises that cannot be kept.

With the overhead of government and the promises of social welfare, our enterprise machine is running out of steam. Taxes are not the answer, because the redistribution of wealth is, in effect, higher taxes, that are not reinvested in the future for any of us. They are wasted on future promises. If we are to fund our evolution and superiority around the world as leaders, not bottom feeders, we must challenge the way our money is being spent. So, indulge me in the following exercise.

Re-Hirement

Darn it's great to be alive
Fending with what life can contrive
Taking it on the chin
Yet keeping a winning grin

I have spent many years in the work hive
Working out the problems of man and wife
Then it all comes down to retire
While keeping a smoldering fire

Only birds pull up from a dive
While doctors are cutting the life line by knife
In view of birthdays help to survive
Beyond the age of seventy-five

Never fear that I'm now here
Calling it rehired rather than retired
Looking for a new career
Wanting my experience to be vilified

In a waning job market and opportunity
My goal is to find a challenge
Not tranquility nor invisibility
So, this trip will test my courage

I must stand up to disappointment
As I approach those who review my resume
And reject my desire for an appointment
Even though I've paid my dues and made my pay

Yes, I'm qualified to be a consultant
As a confidant and problem solver
Companies aren't necessarily solution insistent
On having me as the trigger to their revolver

To cross that line of resistance
For their good and mine we must agree
The cost of hiring me for instance
Depends solely on my value to a company (publisher)

Great to be alive in this bee hive
Where I'm now one of the worker bees
As I make the dive
Into re-hirement
With challenge up to my bended Knees

Aging: Is It a Science or an Art Form?

Studies on the aging process are coming in by the bucket lists. Some studies show an increase in longevity and others that predict obesity and disease will cause the life expectancy to start a sharp decline.

Who is right? What I see are the telltale signs of Americans not taking responsibility for their own health and their ongoing aging costs. What are our responsibilities and what are the tangible and intangible costs of aging?

Responsibilities and current status:

1. Americans need a healthy lifestyle
    a. Fitness: 66 percent of Americans do not exercise even ten minutes per week
    b. Nutrition: 45 percent of Americans do not read the labels on the containers
    c. Emotional Instability: 25 percent of Americans use some form of mind-altering chemicals
    d. Stressors: 90 percent of Americans do not use exercise, relaxation, and meditation in their day
    e. Sleep deprivation: Average sleep is six hours

2. Americans need a healthy financial picture
   a. Serious financial underfunding for the aging costs: most Americans only have Social Security pension benefits with little or no long-term care insurance
   b. No financial plan for nursing home care or declining health costs

Problems: Americans in general do not have healthy lifestyles:

Problem 1: Most Americans ride everywhere. They are generally not fit. Little if no walking is required in our society. Studies show that fifteen to twenty minutes per day of brisk walking will prevent many maladies and improve the longevity by 20 percent. Yet no one walks anywhere unless they have to.

Problem 2: Most Americans eat whatever is put in front of them without regard for nutritional content or side effects on their health. Obesity, a disease of the mind that affects all of the body's functions, is a growing health problem due to the American lifestyle. It is rippling to our next generation.

Problem 3: Most Americans do not get enough sleep and use medication for rest and relaxation.

Problem 4: Most Americans have forty- to fifty-hour-per-week jobs and other time-demanding activities resulting in stressful fourteen- to sixteen-hour days.

Problem 5: 50 percent of Americans are getting divorced.

Problem 6: Most Americans do not prepare for the aging process. Getting old is for someone else, and I will worry about it if it happens to me someday. Studies show there are more young people with diabetes, heart conditions, plugged and inflamed arteries, shortness of breath, osteoporosis, joint diseases, emotional instabilities, social maladies, etc. As these people exacerbate the diseases with weight problems, the hospital and nursing home are not far away.

Problem 7: Most Americans have someone else paying for their insurance and are not responsible for funding the services to treat their poor lifestyles. This builds in overutilization of a cost-based healthcare system. Where treatment is first and foremost with prevention last, if at all. Healthcare is the last profession to be digitized and economized. My book "Health Care for All" explains how this can be done.

Problem 8: The government is administering 80 percent of the healthcare benefits with only 60 percent of the resources needed to pay for an aging and unhealthy population. This is catching up with the state Medicaid programs that now want to ration with managed cost not managed quality care. Medicare is using enforcement and fear to keep their costs down.

Solution: Lifestyles come more easily with a system to follow. Aging needs to be a science rather than an art:

1. There needs to be a personal commitment to health as a lifestyle.
2. There needs to be professional help to set up programs for fitness, nutrition, relaxation activities, vacation, sleep patterns, family counseling for troubles in the marriage, etc. These costs must be controlled and paid for by the individual, not the bureaucracy.
3. There needs to be standardized benefits structured for the personal healthcare needs paid for by the individual, not a remote case manager.
4. There needs to be economic incentives for getting to the above three moral incentives to preserve health and pursue outcomes for unhealthy Americans.

- Tax incentives for investing in a healthy lifestyle
- Tax deduction for fitness center
- Tax deduction for nutritional counseling
- Tax deduction for fitness equipment

- Tax deduction for personal trainer
- Tax deduction for marriage counseling
- Tax deduction for sleep studies and therapeutic devices
- Tax deduction for screening for respiratory, urinary, bone, arterial, mental, and emotional problems
  - Pretax withholding of self-health insurance funding of long-term care insurance premiums for working Americans.
  - Nonworking and underinsured Americans funded through traditional Medicaid taxation programs
  - Elderly Americans that have a need for hospitalization and crisis intervention would be funded through the traditional Medicare taxation programs
  - Providers of health preservation services would be paid on an outcome basis using fitness plan templates and proof of interventions and goals reached
  - Providers of healthcare services would also be paid on an outcome basis using AI care-plan templates and proof of interventions and goals reached for resolving
    - Physical problems
    - Motor problems
    - Emotional problems
    - Social problems

5. Life-expectancy planning and health preservation services then become the mode of managing costs and benefits. They are the new enterprises. Capital investment and return from earnings should be based on outcomes, not everyone's incomes. Right now the life expectancy is a turkey shoot and the costs are fraught with waste and corruption.

6. There is overutilization of the benefits by the unhealthy because the individual costs of health care are external to the person utilizing them and the healthy pay for the unhealthy in the billions of dollars that further destroy the work ethic.

Quotable Quotes

"We used to think there is nothing you can do about aging. You just age. Now there's a feeling that it might be possible to slow it down." Key aging concepts: "Aging isn't a disease, it's a process. You need to know about the biological clock, oxidation, and genes to manage the process." So it is diet for living longer, exercise for living better, and mental balance for living well.

"Slow cooking, not fast food, is the fuel for a longer lasting engine." Fruits, vegetables, red wine, dark chocolate, vitamin E, D, and A, protein replacement, restraint for sugar, salt, white-based products, portion control are for calorie control.

"Exercise is for a smoother running engine." Cardio stimulation, strength training, resistance exercises, aggressive walking, deep breathing, yoga, stretching, meditation. "A study was conducted at a nursing home in Orange City, Florida. Nineteen men and women with an average age of eighty-nine, most of whom used wheelchairs to get around in, did just ten minutes of strength training per week. After fourteen weeks, almost everybody was out of their wheelchairs. One woman moved back into independent living." The results were published in *Mature Fitness*. If this is true for the elderly for ten minutes per week, what would it take to get 20 percent to 30 percent improvement for all ages?

"Use balance of work, relaxation, and sleep for your 168 hours per week: forty hours of work, forty hours of relaxation, forty-eight hours of sleep, forty hours for study and family relationships. When you look at it this way, we have plenty of time for fitness, exercise and wellness activities if we use our time more effectively. Like, put a priority on exercise for living a longer and better life. No excuses accepted.

Never Too Old to Live, Lifestyles for Aging, America in the Red Zone, Elder Pride, How to Live Forever After -health books published by Xlibris, 2012, iUniverse 2009, Lettra Press 2019 www. lifestylesforaging.com www.jerryrhoadsuthor.com

- Jerry Rhoads' self-health book "America in the Red Zone" prescribe making the changes that the Blue Zone principles proposed in the best-selling book The Blue Zones where the author and explorer Dan Buettner chronicles the "Lessons for Living Longer from the People Who've Lived the Longest who with the right lifestyle, experts say, may live up to a decade longer.
- Jerry Rhoads' ten chapters give doable regimens for attaining the ten Blue Zone commandments.
- Jerry Rhoads' tools assist in downsizing your waist size by up scaling your activity to improve your self-worth and BMI.
- Jerry Rhoads' mental exercising as a self-health action is taking your subconscious to task and changing the way you are thinking about yourselves and your lifestyle outcomes.
- Jerry Rhoads' seminars on self-health are taking Americans to Blue Zone status. The goal is to allow us all to break 100.

This book proposes a different approach for aging in America, with proposed structural changes and broader thinking on processes. Without those that are aging and rethinking their life, we are relegated to theories imposed by government. This is the worst possible resolution, with mass numbers of citizens being warehoused in end-of-life care, being rationed out as if they were Soylent Green (remember the 1973 Sci-Fi movie with Charlton Heston recycling aging Americans due to Overpopulation and pollution).

EIGHTY-FIVE PERCENT

I wish I had thought of this
But I learned it from Earle Nightingale
The great guru for the positive list
Of goals that never fail

Eighty-five percent of worries
Are impure thoughts that never come to pass
Eighty-five percent of threat
Is something our mind begets
And the remaining fifteen percent
Is only half as bad as it gets

So why waste away
When only fifteen percent gets in the way
And only half of that
Takes away your other half

Seven- and one-half percent
Won't make a dent
In your future
Or your advent

Eighty-five percent of fear
Is fear itself and a factor
Eighty-five percent of failure
Is in the purpose not the actor

Eighty-five percent of life is attitude
But only fifteen percent know
How to seek its gratitude

Eighty-five percent of the chores are in preparation
And only fifteen percent can withstand the pain

Of the discipline to avoid temptation

Eighty-five percent of planting a good crop
Is in the time it takes to know when to stop
Eighty-five percent of the joy of creation
Is in fifteen percent of the activities that serve our nation

Eighty-five percent of the time is wasted
What a crime
While fifteen percent of the time
We contemplate and whine

Eighty-five percent of our energies are a waste
If we take fifteen percent in haste
And eighty-five percent of the being
Is fifteen percent from what we're seeing

Only a small part of why it takes heart
It takes pain takes effort to grow grain
Cultivate wheat
Find life sweet

And clearly eighty-five percent of the chafe is green
And the other fifteen find life serene
As percentage vintages show the health of the nation
Only fifteen percent of individuals appreciate creation

Adage
No worries, no problems
Eighty-five percent of threat
Is something our minds beget
And the remaining fifteen percent
Is only half as bad as you represent

So clearly 85% of the problems
Our nation faces
Are from 15% of the sins
And not real times and places

Leaving 7.5% as the spaces
In the worries of man
Solved by 85%
Who will say we can

Live fearlessly with staying power

Charter Ten

Give Us Work or Give Us Debt—
Building Ethical Success

W ant   **J** oy
O ffers capital   **O** f
R esources   **B** eing
K indled   **S** omeone
           C oordinates
           A ttitudes
           P romotes
           I nnovation
           T owards
           A ction for
           L everage

We have institutionalized the Enterprise with Big Brother government, public sector dominance, swamped with debt by borrowing our capital. We are dominated by academic issues rather than problem solving. The majority of voters are not empowered to find a reasonable candidate nor party. It is time for the private sector to take back the Enterprise and Capitalize on the resurrected Work Ethic. That's socialism at its best>

The many shall overcome the restrictive rules of the few or we are killing Entrepreneurial spirit and economies in their intent . . .

Adam Smith, *Wealth of Nations*, 1776: "*The general industry of the society never can exceed what the capital of the society can employ. As the number of workmen that can be kept in employment by any particular person must bear a certain proportion to his capital, so the number of those that can be continually employed by all the members of a great society must bear a certain proportion to the whole capital of that society, and never can exceed that proportion. No regulation of commerce can increase the quantity of industry in any society beyond what its capital can maintain. It can only divert a part of it into a direction into which it might not otherwise have gone; and it is by no means certain that this artificial direction is likely to be more advantageous to the society than that into which it would have gone of its own accord.*

The Monopsony Game demonstrating the power of the Government in our lives is available through the American Enterprise Party web site. www.americanenterprisepoliticalparty.org

What is Success?

Is it the man who climbs the highest mountain
Or the woman who swims the widest sea
Or is it the team that somehow wins
Or the person who stands amid fame and fortune
Or is it possible, it's you or me
Let's take a look and see

Are you good at what you do
So you take pride in living
Are you bright instead of blue
And do you get joy from giving

Are you an open book
With passages to be read
Inviting a passerby's look
Even when you're dead

Will your children be proud to say,
"That's my mom and dad
They helped put me on my way
And taught me good from bad"

If you can honestly say, these things
I feel you certainly can confess
That what your life brings
Is an ethical success
At Last

THE END OF THE WORLD

I thought it was the end of the world
But the world didn't end
I thought I was dead to rights
But I wasn't dead

I thought I was guilty
But I wasn't charged
I wanted to hide
But no one was looking

Except fear of my own fear
And doubt which had come to rest
Upon my shoulder
And across my chest

I thought it was the end of the world
But the world didn't end
I thought it was too much to handle
But even that did pass

No more scars than mental anguish
No more suffering did I have to languish
Than thoughts of why I should be giving
The last rites of the end of the world

But the world didn't end

Matter of fact each day
it was on the mend
It was on an upward trend
Though from my perspective

The hill was insurmountable at times

I kept my eye on the target just ahead
Shying away from doubts and dread
But eventually everything worked out
Not exactly with a yell and a shout
But at least things were coming about
So my lesson was to be unbound
If you get down you never know
When that pendulum will turn around

So don't give up and don't count yourself out
Don't give in to fear and doubt
Because the end of the world
Thought to be one-way

Down but never out
Just before it turned about
MAKING AMERICA SAFE AND
FINANCAILLY SOCIALLY SECURE AGAIN
MASA

"Ask not what you can do for your party. Ask what you can do for your party".
To KEEP AMERICA GREAT

The American Enterprise Party Platform

By the Board of Erectors of the Party
www.americanenterprisepoliticalparty.org

For the sake of saving The Great American Enterprise we hereby move and decree

The Articles of Incorporation and Constitutional Bylaws

Mission Statement

For the sake of the nation's survival as a leader in the world, the private sector must take an active role under the laws needed to govern moderate and reformative principles of American enterprises by resurrecting the intent of the American Constitution and by erecting a new political alternative. No longer will the President of the United States and a government of 100 senators, 9 Supreme Court Judges, 435 Congressmen and 22.6 million government employees rule 330 million enterprising Americans without fair representation of enterprising Americans and effective leadership. What is at risk . . . The health and wealth of our nation to be shared, based on individual effort, by all.

ARTICLES OF INCORPORATION

Whereas, the country of America has forsaken the pursuit of happiness, peace, and love of fellow man, and
Whereas, the states have been led by lawmakers who stifle the American enterprise system, and

Whereas, our current public officials are not accountable to the private sector and feel transparency is enough, and

Whereas, the gridlocked (no consensus on any problem) Congress of the United States of America has ground down our national vitality and ability to create jobs and fulfill the American Dream, with burdensome taxes, laws, rules and regulations, and

Whereas, the majority of enterprising Americans want rebirth of constitutional government, we the people hereby erect a new political party founded on the following policies and principles:

1. Practice of humanism bringing capitalism and socialism into the American Enterprise Party political party
2. Humanitarian peaceful coexistence in the world
3. Humanitarian Government by the people, of the people, for the people
4. Less government intervention in all facets of life
5. Recapitalize our American enterprise for its enterprising people
6. Liberate the creators of jobs, knowledge, justice, and the gross national product for all its citizens
7. Restore the health and wealth of America
8. Share in the wealth in proportion to effort and contribution to its making

We as the representatives of the enterprising Americans, who need fair representation, form a contrasting political party that moves America away from great society programs to a freedom to work for the values assured by the American Constitution and to have the following equal rights and opportunities that best serve enterprising Americans and preserve health, happiness, and prosperity for all:

1. Propagate and promulgate family values
2. Pursue STEM and higher education
3. Have home ownership
4. Pursue full employment

5. Have health and wellness services for all
6. Pursue happiness without bias of race, gender, religion or creed
7. Have an opportunity to share in prosperity for all
8. Free to innovate new economies and businesses uninhibited by arbitrary and capricious laws and regulations
9. Support the concept of three-party rule and a swing vote majority

We as the representatives of the American Enterprise Party move and agree to the following health and wealth enterprise platform:

1. Recast the current income tax and estate tax system to recapitalize the American enterprise system based on 5 percent of individual net worth as an equity infusion to refinance the enterprise.
2. Downsize government at all levels by spinning off public services to private enterprise that is accountable to its private sector shareholders.
3. Impose a 5 percent sales distribution fee on foreign sales that utilize the American enterprise consumer market.
4. Pay down the national debt by taxing net worth and eliminating all burdensome taxation that impedes the growth of America's economy.
5. Eliminate the complexities imposed by bureaucratic rules and regulations that turn people against people for inhuman reasons.
6. Turn lawmakers into job makers and peace makers.
7. Improve the health values through Self-Health wellness programs and economic incentives for individuals to have earning their own health annuity by staying well.
8. List all college graduates in a National Job Corps Registry for resurrecting R&D technology for creating enhancements to the American enterprise.
9. Preserve the existing entitlements for the aging and poor by amending Obama Care for the oppressive and costly pursuit of

treating illness. Replacing treatment with the pursuit of wellness outcomes. This paradigm SHIFT can be funded by eliminating the new entitlements for minimum wage, workers comp, unemployment, welfare and guaranteed pensions . . . those being replaced by a system of personal investment accounts reinvested in the American enterprise.

10. Engender the war on debt based on GAAP accounting through reduced deficit spending on weapons of mass destruction, public pensions, perks, and guaranteed compensation packages for the public sector.

11. Resurrect the Keystone Pipeline and form the Great North American Enterprise Union with Canada and Mexico for free flow of immigrants, energy resources, and jobs.

12. Reinstitute off shore drilling and the leases of Federal property for frac king to attain energy independence as attained in the previous administration.

13. Form OPEC (Oil Purchasing Energy Countries) to negotiate with *OPEC (Organization of the Petroleum Exporting Countries)* pricing on oil products to control waste and overutilization of our world's energy resources,

We, as the representatives of working Americans, will dedicate our time to three-party governance at all levels of the American society through reduced dominance of money-driven politics, utilizing the Internet to elect private-sector candidates.

1. Governorships
2. Legislative and congressional seats
3. Mayoral positions
4. County commissioners
5. Township supervisors

The representation and leadership will require a four-year commitment by all American citizens to participate in the reformation of our Founding

Fathers' American enterprise dream. The reformation of America at all political levels must move to:

1. Ensure freedom of speech
2. Freedom of self-preservation and personal defense
3. Freedom to pursue knowledge and opportunity
4. Freedom to determine one's own healthcare and wellness program
5. Freedom to propagate family units regardless of sex, race, or creed
6. Freedom to contribute to foreign relations based on the world's peaceful coexistence and building international relationships and infrastructures for enterprising individuals around our planet.
7. Freedom to practice the principles of humanism for the greater good.

The time has come for the private sector to take back America, the great American enterprise that populates consumerism and allows workers worldwide to form a coalition and consensus of ideas, ideals, and opportunities for all. The war on debt and destruction of human lives for the monetary benefit of the few must give way to a transformation of the government where the involvement of the many will replace the power of the few, where the imposition of money as the flag bearer will give way to knowledge, and the transformation of the world's war on hunger and poverty will be generated by enterprise for job creation and self-preservation, not socialism or any other -ism.
Signed this day of and year

By the Board of Erectors of the American Enterprise Party
                Chairman: Jerry Rhoads
                Vice Chairman: Sharon Rhoads
                Secretary: Alec Stephens
                Treasurer: Kip Rhoads
                Counselor: Mark Levin (proposed AAL)
                Consultant Pro Tim: Donald J. Trump

The American Enterprise Party is based on the proclamation of economic and moral values for the majority of American citizens . . . we hereby revitalize the American worker's jobs for peace not more laws and development of weapons of mass destruction . . . incorporating the mission of building not destroying the fabric of human existence and be the leaders towards a free, healthy, prosperous and peaceful world. Our intelligence and ideals will take us there if we understand that ideas are the fruit of thought and solutions to problems are the result of change and confronting fear thereof.

Twelve-step implementation plan

Timing: after the 20 presidential election and the State of the Union Address, regardless of who wins, we will announce the formation of the party and the ten-step plan with the platform published in Jerry Rhoads' book *"The American Enterprise Party"*

1. Publish the American Enterprise Party Platform Herewith
2. Form the American Enterprise .org corporation
3. Obtain 504 foundation tax exemption status
4. Elect a board of directors
5. Announce the formation of the party in media
6. Sign up participants in the formation of local grassroots members
7. Post videos, blogs, Tweets, and information on the American for Enterprise website on the Internet, announcing the party's platform and objectives.
8. Elicit national press coverage and media coverage for key party members.
9. Announce Jerry Rhoads as the party's candidate for governor of Illinois in 2024.
10. Survey and canvas fifty state governors for their interest and involvement.
11. Sign up key State legislators who represent the private sector for membership.

12. In 2024 have a candidate for American Enterprise Party announce for the presidential race.

American Enterprise Party Platform

(An excerpt from the book *Mancology: The Science of Managing Human Value* by Jerry L. Rhoads, CPA, July 1992, second edition July 2007, third edition July 2012)

Third Party Platform

Operating under the premise that the two-party system in America has narrowed to one party called the *elito-crats*, who govern by the money for the money and not by the constitution. We must go back to the humanitarian government supporting Humanism "for the people, by the people, of the people with life, liberty and justice for all."

1. Authority: the constitutional right of human beings, regardless of color, sex, creed, nationality, or religion to pursue enterprise, morality, happiness, and good fortune,
2. Foundation: constitutional amendments (or executive orders),
   A. All Americans are created to be equal with the opportunity to pursue equality in educational, economic, and religious endeavors.
   B. All Americans have the civil right to an education.
   C. All Americans have the civil right to an enterprise as long as it is pursued with ethics and morality.
   D. All Americans have the obligation to participate in the process of governing themselves if they wish to receive their civil right to an education and economic freedom. This is predicated on the passing of term limits in all levels of government
   E. All Americans have the obligation and responsibility to use guns for protection only and participate in

collecting and banning military weapons for personal use and sale on the open market.

F. All Americans have an obligation to support world peace efforts, utilizing the economics of peaceful coexistence where human value promulgates nonmilitary actions to replace arms buildup and disregard for human life.

H. All Americans have an obligation to practice self-health principles as it is a privilege of self-sacrifice.

3. Structure is founded on *Mancology* as the political and economic philosophy. This is the science of managing human value. The third-party ticket is *Humanitarian,* requiring the direct participation of Americans to accept the responsibility of governing themselves through a modification of the established practices using constitutional law as the catalyst.

4. Strategy of the third party is to offer Americans who believe in the constitutional right of opportunity to participate in establishing a structure (systematic process) that pursues the intent of our Founding Fathers. This strategy will be founded on the following principles:

A. Authoritarian processes will be decentralized in government and business. This is a movement back to the identity of the individual and a movement away from large government and conglomerates who have not met the emotional nor economic needs of the individual.

B. Organizations will be encouraged and taught Mancology so the processes are understood and reconfigured for the benefit of building the skills and productivity of the individual. This will require an analysis of functions and the authority of the individual to produce and effect their own future.

C. Productivity statistics and unitary analysis of cost and benefits of the output versus the input will be posted for all of the functions to review and evaluate.

D. The recapitalizing and financing of government will be based on simplified taxing methods:

 (1) 5 percent flat tax on individual net worth at the Federal level.

 (2) 5 percent tax on corporate and not for profit institutions net worth at the Federal level.

 (3) Zero income tax on individual at the state level, only 5 percent sales tax on individual's consumption.

 (4) 5 percent flat tax on businesses' net worth at the state level, less credits for jobs, investment, research, and development.

 (5) 0 percent capital gains tax, 10 percent investment tax credit at federal level.

 (6) 5 percent investment, jobs, and research and development tax credits at state level.

 (7) 0 percent tax on estates and gift taxes dated prior to new tax system (a $250,000 floor and a $1 billion ceiling); zero estate and gift taxes after net worth recapitalization assessment (tax) implemented.

E. The competitive analysis of the United States in the world market will indicate the value of the individual value and productivity toward national goals. The criteria would consist of:

 (1) Gross national product broken down into the component gross state products that make up the whole

 (2) SAT scores by state

 (3) Employment rates by state

 (4) Crime rates by state (number of guns and shootings)

 (5) Divorce rates by state

 (6) High school graduation rates by state

      (7) Teen pregnancy rates by state

      (8) Literacy rates by state

      (9) Abortion rates by state

      (10) Balanced operating budgets using GAAP

F. The system of financing the American enterprise reinvestment will come from the following changes in the American results:

    (1) Balanced trade deficits (imposition of a 25 percent distribution fee for use of American consumption market to offset the imbalance in pricing in foreign markets).

    (2) Absolving problems requiring American intervention in other countries' internal affairs, except as it directly affects U.S. security.

    (3) Improved worker productivity equating to improved quality and a resultant reduction in the cost of delivered product.

    (4) Emphasis on worker skill development (learn-to-earn programs); this investment in the individual is the cornerstone of Mancology (work ethic).

    (5) Small business financing must be the responsibility of a deregulated banking industry and aggressive tax credits, which promote small-business enterprise as the solution to worker dissatisfaction and unemployment, which is the result of corporate misuse of human value.

    (6) Dissolution of the Federal Reserve Banking system and complete deregulation of banking for small-business private investments.

    (7) Planned and managed integration at strategic border clearing stations of migrants that apply for Social Security numbers, English-speaking

coaching, and apply for citizenship, subject to a waiting period.

(8) Balanced operating budgets using GAAP.

G. A balanced federal budget using GAAP principles through the following initiatives:

(1) Foreign aid phase out for those countries that have a foreign trade surplus with the U.S.

(2) Foreign aid (capital investment in an economic infrastructure) phases up for emerging markets (Mexico, Africa, Middle East, South America, etc.) that commit to peaceful coexistence pledges through the United Nations Security Council.

(3) Realignment of defense spending so it focuses on computerized alert systems and tracking of foreign weapons deployment. Total phase down of the military complex with the objective of more effective foreign policy built on economic power and peace initiatives versus military power being the goal.

(4) Realignment of entitlement programs to the use of enterprise plans and tax credits for SHIFT withholding accounts for self-funding the individual's share of the cost of financing individual healthcare needs and costs.

(a) 100 percent individual tax deductions for health insurance costs.

(b) Job-based tax credits for small business.

(c) Rethinking of retirement age and preservation of Social Security based on personal choice, not a date or an age (sixty-five due to increased life expectancy may be too early). Personal accounts managed by professionals may be a way to disconnect this from government mismanagement of the benefits. (Late retirement versus early retirement may be a cultural change in administering the Social Security benefits.).

(5) Sunshine laws for all legislative programs (pass a bill, kill a bill, review ten other bills for termination or extinction).

(6) Limited terms for congressional seats at state and federal level while discouraging generational nepotism for reelections.

(7) Redistricting of congressional seats based on a revised federal revenue sharing criterion

    (a) Gross state productivity

    (b) State employment rate

    (c) State SAT scores

    (d) State high school graduation rate

    (e) State literacy rate

    (f) State divorce rate

    (g) State crime rate (number of guns and shootings)

    (h) State teen pregnancy rate

    (I) State abortion rate

    (j)   Balanced operating budgets using GAAP

H. Balance state budgets using GAAP principles through the following initiatives:

1. Restructure welfare (great society programs) into great enterprise programs based on "learn to earn" functional job corps to clean up the inner city and instill pride in the traditional neighborhood culture.

2. Institute incentive tax credits for investment in
   A. Full employment job credits
   B. Equal education credits
   C. Affordable housing credits
   D. Capital investment in inner city business
   E. Research and development projects
   F. Mutually-owned health insurance networks
   G. Private Charter educational opportunities for minorities
   H. Drug rehab centers and Planned Parenthood counseling

3. Pass sunshine laws and limited terms for the legislature (for every law passed, an old law must be removed so the funding of the new law can be affordable and ten others reviewed for termination or extinction).

4. Flat tax schedule on individuals of 0 percent of gross spendable income with a 5 percent sales tax on consumable type items.

5. Five percent flat tax on business net worth, less incentive property tax credits, plus a 5 percent value-added tax for financing private education and drug rehab centers and Planned Parenthood counseling, thereby eliminating personal property and real property taxes for funding education.

6. Federal revenue sharing based on each state's
   A. Gross state contribution to GNP
   B. Employment rate
   C. SAT scores
   D. High school graduation rates
   E. Literacy rate

F. Divorce rate

G. Teen pregnancy rate

H. Crime rate (number of guns and shootings)

(I) Abortion rate

(j)   Balanced operating budgets using GAAP

7. Redistricting members of national congress based on the above success contribution formula, getting away from population-related representation and electoral college disparities.

I. National drug management programs administered by states

1. State-financed private investment in drug rehab centers program.

2. State-financed private investment in family counseling centers program.

3. Offer job incentive property tax credits to businesses that assist and employ recovering alcoholics and drug addicts.

J. National prison management programs administered by states.

1. Implement enterprise job-placement incentives to inmates for skill development and release learn to earn programs.

2. Establish private enterprise counseling incentives for institutional rehabilitation and job placement.

3. Offer job tax credits for employment of recovering inmates.

K. National abortion management programs administered by state

    1. Expand sex education and Planned Parenthood through investment in private enterprise counseling centers.

    2. Establish criteria for freedom of choice centers, requiring enrollment in counseling in first trimester (Lower abortions rate).

    3. Establish pro-life and free to choose campaigns focused on sex education and Planned Parenthood counseling.

L. National (universal) healthcare quality control program administered by the private mutually owned health preservation companies specializing in evidence-based medicine and pay-for-outcome processes (utilize a withholding program for individual savings accounts for "aging insurance," with investment and distribution by private enterprise; paradigm SHIFT self-health insurance funding trust to manage the resources).

    1. Disconnect h e a l t h c a r e funding from the employer and connect to individual responsibility incentives. Options for employer equal match).

    2. Set up a standardized health-preservation package of benefits administered by private enterprise (mutually-owned health insurance companies that invest the funding and process the claims) on the basis of the improvement of fitness and the prevention of chronic diseases.

    3. Tax deductions for each individual's long-term care insurance fund. Rates are based on each person's fitness and health profile.

    4. One hundred percent tax deduction to individuals for fitness, nutritional, and weight-

management costs, regular screening exams and annual physicals.

5. Deregulate healthcare providers except for licensure and reimbursement audits. Replace the Department of Health and Human Services with the Department of Quality of Life.

6. Eliminate preexisting-condition clauses and waiting periods.

7. Establish a reinsurance fund for the high-risk pool of individuals who have catastrophic episodes or are underinsured.

8. Do not ration health claims under Medicare and Medicaid programs to critical illnesses for the elderly and the uninsured/underinsured but require that the payment thereof must be based on the basis of outcome, not provider income.

M. National educational management programs administered by the states

1. Standardized SAT scoring.

2. Federal requirement for revenue sharing using an approved curriculum based on 75 percent technical development and 25 percent personal development courses.

3. Graduation rate methodology.

4. Invest in inner city educational reform 75 percent jobs in city enterprises 25 percent personal development for American culture and arts.

5. Counseling for learn to earn, skill to bill, Humancology principles, and local business to rally minorities to nationalism.

6. Encourage the educational focus on the STEM curriculum (science, technology,

engineering and math) and studies but with a more aggressive approach by deregulating the businesses so they can more readily employ such specialized graduates in the pursuit of new technology in the applied sciences and use of liberal arts in the practicum of Enterprise.

Founding principles of Mancology, the science of managing human value replacing capitalism, socialism, racism, ism isms ism's with humanism:

Human behavior: development of the personal being

Axiom one: Humansim values must be learned through traditional family structure and morals exemplified by the parents in the home environment and in the teachings at school and in constructive social agencies for counseling families on such. This is founded on the principle that the value of individuals is the result of each person's constitutional right to pursue happiness and freedom based on their personal commitment to remove all self-imposed obstacles.

The Life and Work ethic is what determines human value in a social sense and it must build on personal worth and a productive work environment. Early retirement is not the mark of a success in America but the value that is brought to the job, and late retirement may mean a more productive and valuable aging process. In this vein, the concept of Social Security may have to be based on an age related to personal decisions, not a specific age or date.

Political behavior: development of political systems

Axiom two: humanism value must be based on the economic realities of our enterprise system. The value of the individual is what each can contribute to the sum total of the society's worth in the world marketplace. This is the gross national productivity founded on the principles of supply side versus demand side economics. The following formulas make up the logic for choosing supply side over demand side economic and political theory:

Demand side economics: Government is expanded to create jobs that do not produce products. The earning power created by these jobs erodes the profits of the businesses through more taxes. The result is less productivity from the workforce because of the emphasis on cost cutting (reduced investment in job training, R&D, and marketing) rather than productivity to meet increasing demand, which would have been created by job training, R&D, and marketing. All of which erodes quality of the input and output units of production. The investments that would result from higher returns do not occur because of the lack of retained earnings, capital, and purchasing power.

This will result in an economic strangulation of resources that America needs to be able to compete in a world economy, that is doggedly in pursuit of the American Dream.

Supply side economics: Government is shrunk to create jobs in the private sector, which produces more and better products at lower costs because of the incentive for workers to earn more and pay less in income taxes. The founding principle here is that less government involvement in business will result in more available profit resources for the expansion of job training, R&D, and marketing of American products to a world economy. The formula is:

<More business deployment>
less government employment =
<More production>
less waste per unit of production =
<More jobs>
less unemployment =
<More quality>
less cost per unit of sales =
<More profits>

less taxes per unit of sales =
<More capital>
less erosion of balance of trade =
<More markets>
less erosion of GNP =
<More resources for eliminating the
budget deficit based on GAAP to pay down debt
<More capital from higher profits and equity =
Balanced operating budgets using GAAP

Disband the term *lawmaker* and replace the process cf lawmaking with peacemakers and job makers. All laws must be economically feasible as well as socially needed so that we do not continue to kill the goose that lays the golden eggs for the sake of the interests of a minority who do not participate in the development and sustenance of the enterprise. We are not meant to be a welfare state but a state with welfare as part of our national responsibilities to the greater good.

Business reform: organizational development for personal change
   Axiom three: Mancology is the science of managing human value for the good of the individual, who will make a commitment to self-development and change of negative attitudes toward their fellow human being. Mancology is a philosophical commitment that the organization's value comes from each of the individual humans that participate in the pursuit of the corporate goals and objectives within the context of each person's goals and subjectives. Thus, emerges the *management by subjectives*, a managerial and political theory that embodies Drucker's MBO and Maslow's hierarchy of individual needs and emotional desires. From this important plank of the platform will emerge sharing in the wealth that is up till now controlled by the elito-crats.

Social reform: personal development for society change

> **Axiom four:** Enterprise is the solution to social and political divergence, which a society needs when the value of human beings is eroded by the destruction of the family unit, social mores and morals, and the sanctity of self-esteem. Enterprise is built on the concept of family values and work ethic.

Constitutional reform: governmental development for nationalism

> **Axiom five:** The American Constitution is the mechanism for change and de-institutionalization of the enterprise system, as regulated by a decentralized government with indicators of human value. The use of unionization for the benefit of the public sector must meet the same criteria as the private sector in using collective bargaining for the benefit of the public domain, not the public officials. Transparency is not enough when the lawmakers become union makers and the enterprise suffers with overloaded fixed overhead and unaffordable benefits for the public sector paid for by the private sector. Put gun control initiatives in the hands of the private sector, not in the hands of politicians, so the elimination of military weapons in the marketplace can be policed and such weapons confiscated.

> Metrics for measuring States government reform effectiveness (ratings from first to fiftieth will be used to allocate revenue sharing):
> - gross state productivity
> - employment rate
> - literacy rate
> - divorce rate
> - SAT scores
> - crime rate
> - teen pregnancy rate
> - inflation rate
> - high school graduation rate

- college graduation rate
- crime rate death by guns rate (number of guns and shootings)
- Balanced operating budgets using GAAP

Political reform: institutional development for democracy

Axiom six: The American Enterprise Party would be managed by Enterprisers who are trained and schooled in the science of managing human value at the local and state level, utilizing the constitution as the guiding text for reform and financial viability in the marketplace. This new political party would run for office at every level, and carry with them the new wave of human dignity—*Mancology*. The third-party candidates would move the country toward a three-party alternative at the state and national level. The governorships and the presidency would be the targets before the senate and house are being represented by Enterprisers so the Party leadership is established first and foremost. Use enterprise as the merger of capitalism and socialism for the greater good becoming the redemption of extremism politics in America.

Axiom seven: Change will be instituted by third party majorities, and not by the traditional special-interest lobbying groups dictating to the Congress what the minority wants for the majority. For the only viable way for America to continue to be a leader in world politics is to demonstrate economically that democracy works and is the direction in which all governments must move in order to improve the value of, and the resulting standard of living of each and every human being.
- Removal of laws when making laws will focus on economics as well as moral and social issues.
- Removal of political campaigns being financed for public hangings on the TV and Internet media . . . debates on problem resolution not just two-party issues are the only topics allowed for public exposure.

- Removal of political contributions being used for public exposure negative campaigns . . . limited to debates and problem resolution that are topical to the voters.
- Removal of generational inheritance of the political office.
- Removal of laws guaranteeing incumbency by redistricting the voters.
- Removal of all laws that deny proof of identity voting.
- Removal all laws allowing harvesting of votes and unmanned drop boxes and unmanned observation posts.
- Removal all laws that prevent validation of voting machine data retrieval and storage.
- Removal of all laws allowing mail-in voting except approved absentee votes within time frame that allows for election night results.
- Amend the constitution for establishing term limits of three years for the House and two years for the Senate.

Axiom eight: SHIFT (Self-Health Insurance Funding Trust) of the paradigm in healthcare to deductive pursuit of outcome from inductive pursuit of treatment based on a method of payment that requires definable outcomes. Physicians, hospitals, nursing homes, home care, hospice, clinics, etc. must be standardized using deductive models of care based on problem assessment, programmatic interventions, and evaluation of outcomes using ISO 10,000 standards. From this paradigm, the use of "evidence-based medicine" and "pay for performance" can be attainable along with transparency, interoperability of data, and control of quality.

- Create a universal healthcare policy for all Americans.
- Actualize the importance of quality of life based on health preservation as a national priority to replace the expediency of sacrificing lives with the following

program of preventing chronic disease, thereby saving cost and lives (amend Obama Care to enact the following principles):

1. Reimburse more for wellness and less for treating illness; take away incentives to keep the elderly dependent and sick.

2. Elimination of "personal spend down" to access Medicaid; do not turn the self-reliant into wards of the state.

3. Federalize Medicaid into a true safety net for the uninsured and underinsured.

4. Standardize Medicare as the true safety net for the elderly and disabled.

5. Initiate personal withholding savings account for long-term care insurance and disconnect funding from employment.

6. Require all healthcare providers practice the Six Sigma principles of eliminating waste through the use of standardized processes, customized care plans, point-of-care computers and the requirement that the patient must be seen before a physician's orders can be given.

7. Provide 50% premium credit reductions for personal fitness, nutrition, health screening, and health-preservation costs expended by each taxpayer.

- Quantify national savings objectives by replacing the current enforcement regulatory system with a re-enforcement system that coaches providers on efficiency, cost effectiveness, quality control, and productivity, utilizing technology and computerized models of care. Eliminate Centers of Medicare/Medicaid and replace with CQL . . . Centers of Quality of life.

Diplomatic reform: foreign policy for development of worldwide commerce

> **Axiom nine:** SHIFT emphasis to Humanism from protectionism and fear to nationalism and peaceful coexistence with the world. The United Nations should be the catalyst to empowering each member to be both enterprising and peacefully conduct business on a worldwide platform. All members sign a pledge of peace and peaceful coexistence with its members and a worldwide plan for financial stability. Any nation not willing to sign this declaration shall not be active in the world marketplace.

- Stop pushing nation building and regime change until there is an opportunity to assist in implementing infrastructure. Allow United Nations to head up banking of resources to assist financially struggling nations rather than the world banking system. Those ready for change can be cloned by the UN for peaceful growth; an entrepreneurial expansion of their legal infrastructure.
- Enable peace corps development of commerce as the solution to terrorism.
- Spend less on arms buildup and more on capitalizing businesses, creating jobs, and market development.
- Develop OPEC (Oil Purchasing Energy Companies) consortium for purchasing petroleum from oil-producing countries. Resurrect the Trump policies and making America energy independent including but not exclusive, the Keystone pipeline, offshore drilling, Federal land leases for fracking and embargoes on Mid-east oil shipments.
- Champion and conduct arms reduction of weapons of mass destruction and outlawing the use of missiles and drones for military purposes.
- Create national and worldwide enterprise (opportunity)

zones and set up local small businesses in all third-world economies.

Election reform: establish proof of citizenship for voting rights with a signature or a mail-in voting justified by a reason not all out chaos with harvesting of votes, uncontrolled drop boxes, no voter ID requirement and late submission and last-minute counts. The Attorney General of Federal and State Justice departments will certify the election results within 7 days of the elections.

> **-Axiom ten:** election reform for security from hacking and altering   results of elections is of the highest priority. The submission of mass mailing coming after the deadline must be rejected so the results can be announced on the Tuesday between November 2nd and 8th every year ... national or local. Observers will be allowed to take notes and report defaults in the protocols. Recounts, if required, have to be finished within 7 days of the election date. Electronic elections must bs managed by the Justice department of each State. Electronic tallying equipment must be certified before each election by the Justice Department for accuracy and security to prevent hacking and alteration of the results. The voting controls must be established State by State through the legislative branch insuring that the election process meets constitutional standards and are responsible for certifying the process before the election and the Attorney General certifying the results after the poles close and before the Electoral College certifies the election.

SUM UP THIS CHAPTER:

If I Were President (a fantasy at my age, since all I run on is my treadmill, but at 81 I can still have this American dream).

It's easy to criticize, hypothesize, visualize, epitomize productive thoughts and opinions. Here's mine … change our culture of violence, vulgarity and excesses to Humanism. So goes the aftermath of the contested election of 2020. Since the country is split into two waring parts as Congress fiddles as America is the victim of overindulgence with an insolvent under pinning.

Therefore, the POTUS' bully pulpit is an enabler to exercise collective leadership and opinion. Since I don't yet have one, I'm going to create my own looking for consensus of ideas, goals and solutions.

First of all, no one is totally ready and competent to be President of a country of 330 million diverse and enterprising Americans. That being the case how can we collectively work together for common goals? What are the collective goals? Are there 330 million different visions of a better world or a consensus of what we all want that becomes our vote to achieve because we passionately need it! Is it a happy family, a healthy lifestyle, a prosperous livelihood, a friendly neighbor, a fulfilling job and a vote that counts?

If it is, listen up because I am going to make a proposition to achieve these individually and collectively to replace what we are now experiencing as a nation of violent behavior, vulgar vocabulary and unequal resources because of unequal opportunity due to poor leaders and poor role models. Our America is a result of just the opposite. Our silent majority are now calling for a change in that culture. Let's review a plan for peaceful change. First, our behavior is our own responsibility so changing that is our personal commitment to change the culture of violence. Secondly, our entertainment is violent and vulgar so why not shut down those instances we all find uncomfortable. Thirdly, is it more money we want or an equal chance at the American Dream of a happy marriage, healthy home and a fulfilling future in our life's work. If it is, how do we get there under the current circumstances?

We are now facing a Pandemic of fear threatening our livelihood and health, along with the changes that our society is demanding of our institutions. These are the result of two- and one-half centuries of development. How can we change these divergent and conflicting goals unless we agree on the changes we want? Do we want a better justice system? Do we want a better health care program? Do we want more resources from our work ethic.? Do we agree that our current leaders aren't taking us there? If so, what can we do? Change our leaders or give in to the current state of affairs? Well, I'm just one voice saying we have to change our leadership regardless of our political affiliation because it is the underlying problem … we have lawmakers making more laws taking away freedoms, the red and the blue defend our establishment binary two-party system, protesters seeding revenge with dark money, defunding our police security blanket, politicians ignoring the blight in our inner cities; effectively breeding crime through gangs as embedded cartel drug dealers in our large and small rural communities while bankrupting our future with financial bailouts.

The problem isn't racism, fascism, capitalism, socialism or any other ism, ism, isms, it's the criminal element and the binary two-party system not honoring Humanism. It breeds a culture of violence, guns, vulgarity in our entertainment (like Roman gladiators killing each other in the name of our own big MARVEL heroes) with the ever-increasing excessive sports heroes' contracts and Big Brother and Brotherhood salaries. Leaving all enterprising workers as spectators of this destructive comedy.

The solution is to pursue Humanism as the national patriotic campaign. It must be driven by the votes of enterprising Americans that pay all the bills, fight all the wars and make capitalists wealthy beyond their dreams and needs … the 200 million enterprising Americans who are not represented nor compensated adequately by a system that glorifies violence, vulgarity and excess compensation in entertainment, sports and our social media. It's the golden rule … those with the gold shall rule.

The vision of a better world would be to create a third political party that pursues enough votes to become the swing vote for every political decision made by the Congress and State Legislators to bring the current proponents of the extremes towards a balanced middle of society. Not left or right, not red or blue, not progressive or socialist, not fascism or communism, but American Humanism. We want to individually have an opportunity to prosper and be happy with our future peaceful dealings around the world including the conservation of our environment and peaceful coexistence with our trading partners and competitors. Read my lips … it's an economic war not a shooting or bombing war. Give peace a chance.

How can this happen. First let's agree on a very important fact. Capitalism is not the enemy of Socialism. They work together every day in every business. I'll call it enterprise and it has to have capital to startup and sustain its equity and it has to have human assets to implement and sustain its profitability. So why do politicians pit one against the other as conservative and liberal, while assigning each to either the left or the right bending the curve towards the extremes for stirring up the voters.

With successful enterprises being the foundation of the American economy, then the extremes of an establishment binary two-party system must be pulled towards the middle-class small businesses that populate our shopping centers, internet trading and commerce with the rest of the world creating standards of living to pay all the bills and taxes to sustain what I call the Great American Enterprise. That's the master we all must serve not 545 people (100 senators, 435 congressmen, 9 supreme court justices and 1 President) who now run everything with money-tics using the golden rule … those with the gold rule. Then humanism creates a new Golden Rule … treat yourself as you treat others… with respect and appreciation of our diverse wants and needs.

The political theory here is to create a swing vote party called the American Enterprise Party that with as few seats as 5 to 10 in the Senate and 10 to 20 in the House representing enterprising hard-working enterprising Americans. I repeat It splits the independents away from the Democrats and the Republicans so neither has a majority. So, a third party does not assure any of the three parties a 51% majority allowing for the filibuster to really mean better legislation and laws.

The third party's platform balances the budget by privatizing agencies that are redundant with all the State Governments and rids every layer of government to "pass a bill kill one standing law and regulations" and taxation becomes a reinvestment of excessive wealth to pay down the unserviceable national and State debt. We not only "drain the swamp" we tame the alligators that are exposed. In a decade, as Margert Thatcher did in England, a third party can kill the idea of bigger government solves social problems and higher taxation pays for it.

AN IDEAIS BORN

What's an idea
A mere flash in the pen
A whimsical panacea
Or just going out on a limb

Might be its thoughts from the past
Or prophecy of the future
But there seems to be no cast
Unto which an idea can secure

Tis probably the searching of the mind
A certain amount of desire
Letting the power unwind
Like adding wood to a fire

Yes raising it to a flame
Fanning and feeding it
Until the past and future are the same
And ideas that seek you
Will become your clever wit

For example's sake let's judge and compare
The electronics that computers make
But still don't care
It's an assimilation for data sake

A match up of past experiences
Organized information and errata
Better senses
The coming together of data

Therefore, the brain
With its own information base
Takes what we know from all time
Relates it to a particular case

And then becomes a thought in the mind
Which sometimes flashes
Sometimes just seems to appear
Fleeting as time smashes
The reason it's here

Those that can grab it in its brief moment
And cup it to their will
Seem to have this summit
Upon which their thoughts fulfill

It's an idea you can kill
Be it theology or psychology
Find that there's no way
To kill an ideology

Give me liberty or give me death
Patrick Henry said
And with this came the lasting idea

That the world upon which he tread
Is the mortal function of theology
Not a passing panacea or folly

By becoming the American ideology
In God we trust
Home of the brave
Land of the free
Liberty for me
From sea to shining sea

Came an idea from the almighty ... a third party

AMERICAN ENTERPRISE

I'm ahead of yesterday
Even if I feel down today
I'm coming over the hill
Though it seems life
Has the taste of a bitter pill

I'm settling down to a routine
Calmest peace I've ever seen
I'm scared
I'll be bored
When my sanity is restored

But still I'm ahead
By being alive not dead
Yes I'm ahead on points
I don't fool around or smoke joints

I'm just a simple enterprising man
Flying somewhere so I can land

And take the rest to my command
Without feeling like I'm making a stand

Where I now band
Ahead of the pack
Taking my back

That's the American Enterprise Party

Jerry Rhoads

THE AMERICAN ENTERPRISE MANIFESTO

As the image shows, I wrote a book entitled The American Enterprise Manifesto that exposes the depth of the swamp and the dire financial predicament this put our country and future generations in. But it must be dealt with now as America slides into the depths of the swamp, fighting alligators not balancing the budget or the Federal debt as did other great societies in the past that failed.

In my opinion, after much research and head scratching, the only way for the gridlock to be broken with an effective swing vote pulling the disagreeable extremes to the middle of the table for problem solving. I've been told it will never happen in America because it takes billions, trillions and zillions to compete for any office let alone the presidency. Well look where money-tics got us ... the swamp is bigger and deeper than the net worth of all Americans combined. Now what? Do we merge with China and hope for leniency on past due interest payments for the imbalance of trade and outstanding Treasury Bills? Or try to give them 100-year replacement "T" Bills at no interest.

Well, 330 million enterprising Americans create $21 trillion GDP per year and create wealth for 16.6 million millionaires and 585 billionaires so why not invest their equity (wealth) in paying down the $158 trillion in unfunded debt, rid ourselves of half of the 22 million government workers that cost 40% of fixed overhead wasted on redundant laws and regulations to be able to compete with China our ominous competitor.

I hope by now, as a discriminating voter, that having a third party representing the Great American Enterprise is a necessity for fiscal and spiritual values of the majority of enterprising Americans. And, it very effectively splits the independents away from the Democrats and the Republicans so neither has a majority. So, a third party does not assure any of the three parties a 51% majority allowing for the filibuster, Electoral College, a swing vote in the Supreme Court and our State legislatures to really mean better legislation and laws. While retaining government by the people, for the people, of the people. With a God of humanism rather then money-tics.

"I pledge allegiance to my Flag and the Republic for which it stands, one nation, indivisible, with liberty and justice for all". To protect our values, constitution and memorials of past heroes of the constitutional government of diversity and ethnicity.

IVORY TOWER

When I worked for an accounting firm we called
Pe final say the ivory tower

Abuse of the seat of power
Sitting in an ivory tower
Away from the humdrum and the cower
Just sitting on the seat of power

Misuse of status
Abuse of the right to lead honestly
What a mess when it's not about us
And the seed to integrity

Pe stem of competence in spite of fear
And the roots of principles held true
So your honor is what we need to hear
Not just the praise you

Abuse of the seat of power
Is sitting in the ivory tower

Sifting platitudes out of the shower
Believing only what you're told
Looking in the mirror with face of dower
Never venturing outside the fold

Pe fold of isolation at the top of society's gradation
Just to feel the height of adulation
Ah you say that is the leader's station
He's above and beyond the ordinary creation

For if he were to stand down on the lower
Alongside the peasant and the poor

Waiting for their score
Anticipating what is in store

He might just have to accept reality
And understand why there's history
Feeling what it's like to just be
Overwhelmed by mediocrity

But no there is abuse of the seat of power
More for the high that it brings
From the isolation in the ivory tower
Like a kite without strings

Just flying high saying look at me
Not stopping to make a mental note
Pat in the land of the free
I'm the reason poor people cast their vote

It is not to jack me up on this seat
It was to provide a semblance of leadership
So they could admire the importance of my feat
Being the captain or the helmsman of the ship

Yes it was someone to admire
More than the ordinary can perceive
But not so high or higher
As to be out of touch and deceive

Because when the seat of power is out of touch
Pen there is abuse
And there's no in between to provide a crutch
For the taint of the mortal recluse

With the abuse by a Sam Rayburn
To go along to get along with a liar
Yes oh yes that's my concern
Burn down that ivory tower

Cast your vote
Cast out that seat of power
Choose a leader for the boat
Hear ye extricate the ivory tower

Vote with your gut
For if you happen to pick a goat
With your head or butt
We shall all end up in the moat

With collective voting the dower
Of the people, by the people, for the people
A populous shining its power
Void of the ivory tower

And its failure to empower
Pe higher power ... to the people

FINAL WORD

Laissez Faire … a lifestyle of Work Ethics

My health care books listed in the Other Titles are primarily about the poor health of Americans. In effect America's collective health is the biggest and most immediate problem. Read my lips it's our lifestyle habits and work ethics that need to be priority over climate change, so called systemic racism and the cold trade war with China. When we win the goal of being number one in the world with life expectancy and number one if cost per capita we will win the other wars with our patriotism and humanism.

America, despite the cost and effects of the corona virus, is the largest health service provider in the world with the highest per capita costs and is rated thirty-eight in quality. The "Boomers are Coming" exacerbates the problems of the Government's dysfunctional health systems. It's about the 117 million people with at least one chronic disease. It's about the failure of Government run health care, the VA debacle and the underfunding of Medicare and Medicaid that's destroying the very fabric of Americans' lives. This is clearly evident as Americans panic to an over reacting worldwide Corona Virus pandemic likely released as a strategic biological synthetic chemical weapon by China.

Currently, health care funding is a $4.2 trillion annual cost (add $9 trillion dollars with the pandemic), political football. Proposals from both parties are suspect since they aren't based on performance or outcome. Medicare for All, the Public Option, Obama Care, Trump Care, private insurance do not deal with prevention as a policy or have health preservation as an objective. It is treatment and medication driven. It is estimated that the prescription drug business in America accounts for $600 billion to $900 billion per year (growing at the rate of 25% per year (just look at the dirge of pharmaceutical commercials pitching pills not prevention) in contributing to an overdosing society.

With Children on Redlin, teenagers on opioid pain medications, middle agers on opioids, statins and blood pressure meds, and old agers on oxycodone, fentanyl, blood thinners, psycho tropics, blood pressure and cholesterol medications lowering life expectancy for the first time in history, not improving it, preserving it or preventing pandemics.

This is being exacerbated by The BABY BOOMERS who are retiring at an unrelenting speed of 10,000 per day and applying for Medicare at 7,000 per week into a health care system that costs $4 trillion per year that cannot handle the three million currently needing health care services. So, a shift in the paradigm to a technology driven self- health care is inevitable. This cuts illness costs and improves wellness outcomes.

The cost of illness escalation is eating up national resources faster than we can cover them. The average cost of an outpatient procedure in a hospital is more than $15,000 . . . inpatient $100,000 . . . a month's stay in a skilled nursing home $7,000 . . . a year over $60,000 . . . a monthly stay in assisted living $6,000 . . .cost per hour for accountants servicing health care $300 per hour . . . attorneys $500 per hour and malpractice claims in the millions . . . Hospice care $700 per day . . . Home care $1,000 per day . . . when is it going to stop! At the same time Society is gaining weight at an astounding rate, there are over 2.5 million falls per year for aging Americans, there are 8 billion pills passed to aging Americans in nursing homes, there is $50 billion dollars per year spent on enforcing and avoiding the intrusion of Government regulations, there are $1 trillion in Obama Care for the inclusion of funding for academic demonstration projects over the next 10 years to supposedly improve quality of care and life of the aging Americans and another $1 trillion dollars in the next 10 years for enforcement of the Affordable Health Care Act by the IRS.

According to studies there are not enough primary care physicians now let alone the 12-multiple looking us in the face for doctors, nurses, therapists over the next 10 years to treat escalating illnesses. The Government in all their lack of vision has restrained the development of nursing home beds for the last 20 years with plans of keeping the sickly elderly at home with relatives. Bleak as it seems these problems need solutions or we will all be at home taking care of the sick and dependent relatives. Instead of academic testing we need entrepreneurial outcomes creating savings.

That's the bad news. Here's the good news. The Great American Enterprise is thriving on its momentum. However, as we have learned in the first two volumes our priorities are off kilter due to poor leadership by both parties. The solution for the health care problem is termed self-health. Following are the principles of self-health covered in Volume two.

1. Shift the Paradigm to Self-Health programs (SHIFT) for preventing chronic illnesses, obesity and depression by privatizing the funding to Self-Health Funding Trusts.

2. Reduction of chemicals and prescription drugs ingested by Americans.

3. Physical and mental exercising that fights off obesity and depression.

4. Self-Health preservation initiatives by health and fitness experts. Jerry Rhoads 5. De-institutionalization of the elderly and disabled.

6. Natural health remedies promoted and provided by health professionals.

7. Most importantly resources used to pay for outcomes not incomes . . . define outcomes as the reduction of known health and illness problems not just symptomatic guesses or medical diagnosis without root cause analysis.

To accomplish this, Health service providers will have to base their services on each individual's health-fitness genetic profile using artificial intelligence (AI) computer models of care with anticipated outcomes for individualized problems. Each service provider would be paid on an economic incentive formula for improving wellness and each American would pay premiums based on their health-fitness genetic profile. Those unemployed or dependent upon the government will continue to receive Medicaid benefits. But a better solution is to attack the squaller in the inner cities and small underserved communities that also breed crime at a higher rate, with the self-health program of prevention and preservation of the individual's health for the greater good in battling our other national priorities ... namely China and bio warfare.

What are the five chronic diseases and cost of care killers?

- Diabetes
- Obesity
- Cardiovascular disease
- Hypertension
- Lung disease What is the cost of chronic diseases?

The CDC forecasts that forty-three percent of the health care expenditures are spent annually on chronic diseases. That translates into $860 billion spent after the disease is active and tight as a noose. What can we do to prevent rather than just treat chronic diseases? Fitness: prevents or avoids chronic diseases Studies have given physical fitness high scores on building immune systems and warding off chronic illnesses and pandemics.

For example, the use of cardiovascular training equipment builds the cardio system to preserve health and build the immune respiratory system. Nutrition: prevents chronic diseases Studies have shown that a proper diet of fiber, fruits, vegetables, and white meat builds resistance to heart problems, cancer due to carcinogens, obesity, and diabetes, Avoidance of harmful chemicals: prevents chronic diseases Studies and history have shown that cessation of smoking and use of illegal, nonprescription and some prescription drugs, and alcohol allows the body to sustain its immune system without dependency on chemicals. Positive relationships: prevent chronic diseases Studies and experience has proven that a stable relationship with a companion removes and can eliminate stresses in life decisions, thereby preventing chemical and food abuses and preserving the body and mind through positive reinforcement of self and attitude.

This converts to a stronger mind and body for building and preserving the immunity to chronic diseases. Meaningful family values: prevent chronic diseases The family unit remains the most stabilizing force in Americans lives regardless of age. Even though the divorce rate (50% of new marriages HEALTH CARE FOR ALL: SHIFT the paradigm from INCOME to OUTCOME for the greater good and 2.4 million Americans get divorced annually) has complicated the process, the nuclear family still prevails as the most important factor in warding off weaknesses of the body and the mind.

Not only does this affect the health of America, it affects the very future of our economy. Spiritual commitment to self and others: prevents chronic diseases. It is simply mind over matter. "You are what you think you are." "Do unto others as you would have them do to you." "If you can conceive it, believe it, you can achieve it." These quotes all revolve around faith and spiritual values that preserve our health. If you cultivate your spirit, you will grow strong physically, mentally, socially, and spiritually.

What an indestructible combination of life builders! The immunity of the self and others to chronic illness thrives on belief and hope—these are the cure-alls for the mind to ward off the weaknesses of the body. AKA Preventive Chronic Diseases are the Problem Demanding a Solution!

Summary: Since it has been shown that the above principles are true and will reduce the stranglehold that chronic disease has on our aging population, let's explore what we, the people, can do to preserve the health of all beings, and at the same time save the dollars that are being spent on chronic diseases. The paradigm must SHIFT from health care to chronic disease prevention and health preservation as the prevailing obligation of health care professionals for the cost and quality benefit of all Americans. Economically, this can be accomplished simply by rewarding the compliant American with benefits that the noncompliant has to earn … not a sin tax but a life time reward of longevity and happiness in marriage and work. A very effective and economic cost of self-preservation.

LIFESTYLE HABITS

Only if I had another life to live
Happy birthday would be my time to give

But talk is free
Health isn't granted
Time is taken
Habit isn't planted

Pride is stilted
Death is sudden
Where my vow is jilted
I'm never too young for heaven

Lifestyles call collect
And expect fulfillment
As we play at life so we can expect
To live and pay by slowing decent

Pere's no compromise to make it work
Not even work equals time missed
If our personal perspective we shirk
Reality is poor lifestyle habits to resist

To pursue our dreams
Our pleasures over the blues
As illusive treasures it seems
Lifestyles are fruits of "free to choose"

No Bourgeois
No politburo
No Pird Reich
No Mafia
No KKK
In our way

No inhibition to live
And let live
To try
And let die

Except the golden rule
"In a lifestyle chosen
We can bluff and free a fool
With inhibitions he thought frozen"

Letting life warm the highs
Before the opportunity dies
By saving lives without demise
Read my lips it's the style not the size

Pe self-healthy lifestyle is a second chance
at happiness and longevity in disguise

SELF-HEALTH DIET DEFINED You are the only one that can determine your lifestyle and life time… unless you get shot by your own gun … so the definition of Self-Health is the most important information you can receive. Many Americans use self-help diet plans to feel better, think better but never are better … so I have coined the term SELF-HEALTH DIE-T … which means you use any unnatural diet you will DIE-TOO soon:

S cience

E ngineered

L ife

F ulfillment

H ow you think determines your weight and longevity

E at when you are hungry and stop when you're full

A ge isn't the right measure of your longevity

L ife is to enjoy and make the most of it by living stronger

T ime is a factor in your use of it living longer

H ealth is a journey not a destination

The human spirit formula: Mentally and physically healthy…Body… Mind…Heart…Soul …Brain = Self-Health

If we follow our conscious minds, we will never find true happiness due to acquired habits and attitudes. So, Self-Health starts with the subconscious mind by stop thinking about failure and start controlling your thoughts through mental exercises that will enable you to accept and enjoy physical exercises. These are called affirmations and confirmations stated to yourself in the quiet times. Physical and mental health start with human value and ends with happiness, prosperity and longevity.

When these thoughts become lifestyle habits, you will find guilt only in the habit of putting them off. "I do not love working out I only feel fulfilled by the act of doing it" … said Jack Lalanne … the Godfather of Fitness" who lived healthy, happy and prosperous until he was 96.

The bottom line is self-health and the finish strong line is 100 chronological years old with a biological age of 10 TO 20 years less. Given the scientists prediction an average life expectancy in 100 years will be 120+. To get there many habits have to change and each individual will have to manage their own health care costs … thus self-health will become the new self-help culture. **And the American dream will embrace the human spirit as the essence of infinity and laissez faire.**

HUMAN SPIRIT IS INFINITY

What is the first and last life form on earth ... the earth worm
And the atom and eve called our spirit

No matter how we step on earth
Ravaged or a tragic birth
It's only the beginning

Beginnings with no predictable end
With only wounds to mend
And minds to bend

Like the trail of the wind
It shall blow where it's asked to blow
Will go where it must go

Originals are only the beginning
Virtues only needed for the sinning
With games played only for the winning

Progress would mean nothing
Unless Picasso's talent had a student
And someone to retort what Shakespeare meant

We're only the beginning
Lo the legends are spinning like a bottle
Holding on to the throttle

And soon will point to the birth
Bringing perpetuation to the earth
For this reason, history shall expand its girth

And infinity shall be a word
To explain why we can touch the sky
And the good shall never die

But what does this mean
This so-called eternal scheme
Of the start and the stop to redeem

It's truly the offspring
Of an immaculate Queen bee birth
That gives girth to we humans on earth

So we could wonder
Why the King gave rise to his son
So his life could strategically be done

So we could take charge of our sins
Despite the crushing winds
With yesterday and today as our friends

Beginnings with no ends
Yes birth is just the beginning
The originals are just for amends

The genius the maestro the brilliant star
Are all trappings
With each of us being what we are

Cells and atoms revolving afar
With a spirit able to traverse
Into the infinite universe

In the beginning there was energy
In the end there is energy
It has been and will always be

A lifestyle of work ethics and civility
Proving that the human spirit is infinity

Laissez Faire … a lifestyle of Work Ethics

LAISSEZ FAIRE
Is America the land of laissez faire not lazy faire?
Yes, where the objective monetary capital marries the subjective
Human capital it gestates the great American Enterprise to create
infamy …

Laissez faire
Abstention of government
Unrestraint of trade
Free enterprise
Free trade
Free-market capitalism
Free lifestyles and work ethics

Leave that entrepreneur alone

What is Laissez faire … is it?
Economics American style
With ethical work
Controlled by capital
Controlled by workers
Controlled by corporations
Controlled by government
Controlled by seller … a monopoly
Controlled by the buyer … a monopsony
Or only controlled by destiny

Or is it Lazy faire?
Control by Congress
90% attorneys
Lawmakers
Regulators
Givers or Takers

Squeezing out the
Market makers
Business shakers
Criminal factors
Immigrant slackers
Foreign hackers

The balance is in jeopardy
Being twisted by regulators
Being pounded by dissenters
Being grounded by speculators
Being questioned by Senators
Being challenged by legislators

Let's save the Great American Enterprise

Will it be the Blue party ... no
Will it be the Red party ... no
Will it be the independent party or the tea party ...
Capitalism Socialism ism ism
Who or what will it be????

How about Humanism and enterprising workers

Ask the 200 million enterprising workers
Who pay all the bills
46 different taxes and growing
Carrying 40% Government overhead
Heaped on small business costs
The Federal Reserve is unfettered
Creating a debt driven economy
And a derivative bubble
Creating economical trouble

Well, we don't have Laissez faire
We have lazy faire
Unemployment compensation

Food stamps
Workers' comp - Disability claims
Paid leave
Illegal workers
Stimulus pay to play
Billions and zillions to play politics
All the new entitlements
Are the demise of the
>*American standard of living*
>*American work ethic*
And the American Dream

With the real entitlements in jeopardy
Medicare and social security aren't to count
To be called so makes no sense it isn't free
It's our money in a personal savings account

To save the true entitlements
How about electing
Someone like a humble Donald Trump
And fifty governors who represent
The Great American Enterprise
And call it the American Enterprise Party

With a voting bloc of
200 million workers (including 30+ million immigrants)
77 million baby boomers
40 million independents
40 million AARP members

If you agree join today
The American Enterprise Party
A political party for Laissez faire

(Dedicated to the axiom "Lazy isn't Faire)

*Making **A**merica the **L**asting **G**reat **E**nterprise (**ALGE**)*

(Exhibit F Volume Two for eliciting your opinion for what is a problem versus just an issue to be tabled and call for reform, a classic political stall tactic so the voters forget how that problem was squelched or perverted into a law with regulations that take away our freedoms) **"Being politically correct is to go along to get along", Sam Rayburn and President Biden saying "no worries" and appease our enemies. But being humanly correct "is getting along to go along to get along", Jerry Rhoads author, founder, CEO of the American enterprise Party.**

MISTAKES *A*VOIDED

A mistake avoided is better than guilt exploited

Two years from today (Biden)
Two years back from yesterday (Trump)
What a difference time will make
For divergence is a mind's mistake

Two years ago, it wasn't so
What I now know
Two years hence
Is wistful suspense

But as amazing as it may seem
Two years can confirm a dream
It can make you glad
It can make you sad

Just on the thoughts you've had
Two years from today
Two years ago yesterday
Is a glimpse of time's decay

But a long look at the past
That I thought was happiness

Is trying to make today last
With a healthy future within my grasp

But it just wouldn't stand still
Even though the casing fit my will
Eluding me like a butterfly
Leading me on the more I try

Till I took a step back
Contemplating what I must lack
Justly I began to look forward
With my sight in accord

For life's true target
Thinking what I would bet
Would be what I would get
Not regret

I visualized I memorized
I've been almost hypnotized
So whatever I wanted
Before my eyes undaunted

Kept me wondering
Can dreams come true or be recounted
Why and how can that free me
Is success what we see flaunted
Only available to some of us in some degree

For if current actions towards illusions
Heal the contusions
And soothe the soul
Why do we chase a futile goal?

What a difference time will make
Two years from a mistake (Biden)

For right has no calendar (Trump)
Nor does happiness come to a bystander

Two years from today (bigger isn't better)
Two years ago yesterday (smaller a go-getter)
Happiness is never far away
Since the future shall relive the dues we pay

And the mistakes avoided as we pray
Be it the party we vote in
Or the party we condemn
Problems require solutions today

Red or Blue
Left or Right
Me or You
We fight the fight
The time is right
To have a swing vote

American Enterprise Party
www.americanenterprisepoliticalparty.org

AUTHOR'S BIO

Jerry L. Rhoads, the author has extensive experience in all facets of health care. He was a consultant that helped implement Medicare and Medicaid in hospitals, clinics, nursing homes and long-term care campuses. He was licensed as a Nursing Home Administrator in multiple states and has managed urban, suburban and rural health care facilities. He is a CPA and a graduate of Simpson College, in Iowa. He, his wife and son owned two skilled nursing facilities in Iowa and one in Arkansas. He has invented, with the help of his son, Artificial Intelligence (AI) software for managing the restorative processes for the elderly so they can be returned to the community. The author has also been consultant to State and Federal Government for devising payment methods for health care providers and served on numerous committees developing legislation for long term care and testified before legislative committees as an expert witness.

The author has worked for a large public accounting firm, been a partner in two others and has owned and successfully run his own businesses for 37 years. During that time, as an entrepreneur, he started a CPA firm specializing in health care and added management consulting and software development to the services offered principally to nursing homes and small hospitals. Over the years his expertise in Medicare and Medicaid led him to representing long term care Association members in proposed legislation and quality improvement methods for the operators of those small businesses.

He has written extensively and presented seminars and national workshops in 22 different states. He has six books published on the subject that he terms Self-Health books, proposing that the solution to funding America's declining health and escalating cost is to have each individual be responsible for making their own health and welfare decisions. By using funds set aside for them in investment withholding accounts they can make their own decisions in preserving their health while preventing chronic diseases that currently rage nationwide. Of course, without a better method than Obama or Biden Care, funding the health care benefits for 77 million baby boomers will result in rationing their benefits to younger populations and therefore, the elderly will not receive their entitled Medicare benefits they've paid for.

Jerry and Shari, his wife of 61 years now live in Chicago, Illinois after being displaced to Iowa from 2009 to 2015 reversing their culture shock back to Iowa and Arkansas to run their three skilled nursing homes (small businesses) with their son. In their 70's they started a new business of restoring the elderly and disabled back to their homes. . . a new version of nursing home care termed Restorative Care. After seven years of fighting with the regulators over how their All-American Care restorative model positively changed the environment and quality of life for their patients, they sold them and they were turned back into warehouses by corporate chain operators.

They have four grown children, twelve grandchildren and five great grandsons and four great granddaughters so far. Jerry and Shari believe that middle America is and has been by far the greatest place to live after having consulted with nursing homes in 22 different states dealing with the most regulated business of all time . . . nursing homes. It is their mission, through this book and his other health care books, to change the punitive and negative disincentives that exist in the Federal and State survey process to a reinforcement approach that allows the small businesses to direct their own version of quality of life not just bureaucratic, arbitrary and capricious interpretations of the quality of care.

This will require that the payment methods also be changed to performance-based reimbursement using add-on programs and quality incentives utilized by the state of Illinois in the 1980's that Jerry helped design and implement. For complete coverage of this proposal refer to Jerry's book "Health Care of All" (How to Fix Nursing Homes and Prevent Pandemics) published by Page Turner Press, 2021.

LIST OF SOURCES

- Google Search engine

- Wikipedia search engine

- Orlando Sentinel 2011 article by Charles Reese "Who is the gang of 545 vs. 330,000,000 People (100 Senators, 435 Congressmen, 9 Supreme Court Justices and 1 President)"

- Affordable Care Act of 2012 (Obama Care)

- Medicare regulations

- George Orwell books ("1984" and "Animal Farm")

- Adam Smith book "Wealth of Nations"

- Aldous Huxley book" A Brave New World"

- US Constitution citations

- Epoch Times reports regarding China

- Dennis Prager quote

- Jerry Rhoads podcast "American Enterprise Manifesto" 2020-21

- Jerry Rhoads quotes, poems, books and articles

- Margaret Thatcher quotes

- Ronald Regan quotes

- John Lennon lyrics

- www.usdebtclock.org

- www.americanenterprisepoliticalparty.org

- Lee Drutman article for the National Constitution Center "Breaking the Two-Party Doom Loop: The Case for Multiparty Democracy in America"

- Linda Killian, book "The Swing Vote", St. Martin's Press, 2011

- China's Economic Council long and short-term plans

- Center of Disease Control quote 2020

- Federal Disease Administration

- New York Times quote 2020

- Governor Cuomo quotes

- "American Enterprise Manifesto" book published by Xlibris 2012, author Jerry Rhoads

- "Health Care for All" book published by Page Turner Press 2021 author Jerry Rhoads

- USA government budgetary information and statistics

- Marianne Williamson, author of book "The Healing of America"

- John Streusel quotes 148

- Karl Marx German Philosopher and author of "Communist Manifesto", 1843

- Be Stein quotes

- President Biden's Executive Orders, 2021 149

OTHER TITLES AUTHORED BY JERRY RHOADS
(Available in book stores and on Amazon.com)

- Health Care for All (How to Fix Nursing Homes and Prevent Pandemics) (a self=health book)

- How to Stay Married Forever After (12 vows/habits to live by: forever after) (a self=health book)

- Life Styles (Of the Healthy, Happy and Prosperous) (a self=health book)

- Never Too Old to Live (a self=health book

- America in the Red Zone (a self=health book)

- Restore Elder Pride (a self=health book)

- Remedy Eldercide (a self=health book)

- The Monopsony Game (an economic analysis)

- Failing Government Taketh Away (a political analysis)

- American Enterprise Manifesto (a third political party proposal)

- Basic Accounting and Budgeting for Long Term Care Facilities

- Americana 1984 2084 2184 (a novel remembering George Orwell)

- Mancology (the science of managing human value)

- Cost Accounting for Long term care facilities

- The Eighth Wonder of the World (first Wonders poetry book)

- The Ninth Wonder of the World (second Wonders poetry book) The Tenth Wonder of the world (third Wonders poetry book)

- The Eleventh Wonder of the world (fourth Wonders poetry book)

- The Twelfth Wonder of the World (fifth and final of the Wonder series)

JERRY L. RHOADS, CPA, GOVERNMENTAL CONSULTANT

My expertise is in the following business models:

CPA firms, Software developer, Management consulting in long term care, Nursing Home Management, Skilled Nursing Home ownership, Published Author in genres of health care, costing long term care, poetry, novelist, Self-Health, Self-Help, a political third party.
Companies: All-American Care, J.L. Rhoads & Co., CPA firm, Rhoads HealthCare Consulting, Management and ownership. Word Data Processing, software developer, Rhoads Limited Partnership, a tax shelter partnership, MBO Management By Objectives, Cost Report Consulting, ROSE Rhoads Offers System Excellence Profession Group, ROSE Systems, Inc., Rhoads Offers Systems Excellence, MRT Maximum Reimbursement Technology. ROSE Systems implementation.

Founder and CEO of the www.AmericanEnterprisePoliticalParty.org, a third political party, representing a swing vote in America can politics. Supported by Mr. Rhoads' American Enterprise Party Trilogy. Volume one why a Swing Vote for Humanism, Volume two Enterprise Manifesto, how to Keep America Great, Volume three, Restore the patriotic, and ethical world ethic.

You can find him via Spotify as a podcaster, The American Enterprise Swing Vote Party, his blogs with the same link, www.jerryrhoadsauthor.com, www.allamericancare.com.
www.lifestylesforaging.com presenting a memoir with his wife of 64 years,
jerry.l.rhoads@gmail.com.
BOOK TITLES AUTHORED BY JERRY RHOADS (Available in book stores,
www.jerryrhoadsauthor.com, www.jerryrhoadsbooks.com and on Amazon.com):

Health Care for All (How to Fix Nursing Homes, and Prevent Pandemics)\(a self-health book).
How to Stay Married Forever After (12 vows/habits to live b, :forever after)(a self-health book).
Life Styles (Of the Healthy, Happy, and Prosperous)(a self-health book).
Never Too Old to Live (a self-health book.
America in the Red Zone (a self-health book).
Restore Elder Pride (a self-health book).
Remedy Eldercide (a self-health book).
The Monopsony Game (an economic analysis).
Failing Government Taketh Away (a political analysis) .
American Enterprise Manifesto (a third political party proposal).
Basic Accounting and Budgeting for Long Term Care Facilities.
Americana 2184 (a novel revisiting George Orwell's 1984).
Human Cology (the science of managing human value).
Cost Accounting for Long term care facilities.
The Eighth Wonder of the World (our amazing human eternal mind).
The Ninth Wonder of the World (our amazing human eternal brain).
The Tenth Wonder of the world (our amazing human eternal soul)..
The Eleventh Wonder of the World (our amazing human eternal heart).
The Twelfth Wonder of the world (our amazing human eternal spirit).
Coming soon:
The Thirteenth Wonder of the world (our amazing journey thereafter).

JERRY RHOADS PUBLISHING 2024

www.ingramcontent.com/pod-product-compliance
Lightning Source LLC
Chambersburg PA
CBHW041041050426

42335CB00056B/3196